Parenting Adhd

Parenting Girls and Raising Daughters to Live a Life With High Self Esteem

(Parents, Toddlers and Discipline)

Gerard Brown

Published by Rob Miles

© **Gerard Brown**

All Rights Reserved

Parenting Adhd: Parenting Girls and Raising Daughters to Live a Life With High Self Esteem (Parents, Toddlers and Discipline)

ISBN 9781990084348

All rights reserved. No part of this guide may be reproduced in any form without permission in writing from the publisher except in the case of brief quotations embodied in critical articles or reviews.

Legal & Disclaimer

The information contained in this book is not designed to replace or take the place of any form of medicine or professional medical advice. The information in this book has been provided for educational and entertainment purposes only.

The information contained in this book has been compiled from sources deemed reliable, and it is accurate to the best of the Author's knowledge; however, the Author cannot guarantee its accuracy and validity and cannot be held liable for any errors or omissions. Changes are periodically made to this book. You must consult your doctor or get professional medical advice before using any of the suggested remedies, techniques, or information in this book.

Upon using the information contained in this book, you agree to hold harmless the Author from and against any damages, costs, and expenses, including any legal fees potentially resulting from the application of any of the information provided by this guide. This disclaimer applies to any damages or injury caused by the use and application, whether directly or indirectly, of any advice or information presented, whether for breach of contract, tort, negligence, personal injury, criminal intent, or under any other cause of action.

You agree to accept all risks of using the information presented inside this book. You need to consult a professional medical practitioner in order to ensure you are both able and healthy enough to participate in this program.

Table of Contents

INTRODUCTION 1

CHAPTER 1: THE TODDLER–A CURIOUS LITTLE PERSON 3

CHAPTER 2: HOW TO SMARTLY SET THE LIMITS 11

CHAPTER 3: HOW TO TALK TO YOUR TODDLER 18

CHAPTER 4: HITTING, KICKING, AND BITING 38

CHAPTER 5: RAISING A CREATIVE CHILD 55

CHAPTER 6: RESPONSIBILITIES OF AN ADULT 59

CHAPTER 7: MEANING OF LONG-DISTANCE PARENTING . 70

CHAPTER 8: SIMPLE WAYS TO BOOST SELF-ESTEEM 75

CHAPTER 9: SELF-DEVELOPMENT FOR A MODERN KID 82

CHAPTER 10: PEACEFUL, PATIENT, AND POSITIVE PARENTING 92

CHAPTER 11: SINGLE MOM WITH TODDLERS - HANDLING TEMPER TANTRUMS 100

CHAPTER 12: MINDSET 109

CHAPTER 13: CONFIDENT CHILD 119

CHAPTER 14: UNDERSTANDING YOUR DAUGHTER 128

CHAPTER 15: YOUR TEEN'S RIGHT TO MAKE CHOICES ... 136

CHAPTER 16: WE ALL HAVE BAD HABITS 141

CHAPTER 17: TIPS ON BEST CAR SEAT POSITION 147

CHAPTER 18: HOW TO DEVELOP A STRONG-WILLED CHILD 153

CHAPTER 19: SETTING BOUNDARIES AND RESPONSIBILITY 156

CHAPTER 20: TAKING THE ASSISTANCE OF THERAPISTS OR SPECIALISTS.. 170

CHAPTER 21: HOW DO I HELP MY TEENAGER NAVIGATE RELATIONSHIPS (FRIENDS, FAMILY, DATING, ETC)?....... 176

CHAPTER 22: YOUR CHILD'S LEARNING DEVELOPMENT 181

CONCLUSION.. 190

Introduction

The step parent is an untouchable. There are years of shared history, recollections, association and encounters between individuals from the organic family that the step parent will never be a part of. Obviously in time the step family will develop into something new and great, however, first there will be a touch of trade off.

Being the second spouse/husband/critical individual has advantages, the fundamental one of which is that your partner as of now has a practical thought of the work that is required to make a marriage work. There are no illusions the second time around in connection to the marriage, however, there might be a couple in connection to the family.

The uplifting news is that there are things that should be possible to smooth the blocks along the way regardless of the fact that you cannot totally get rid of them.

In a step family, everybody accompanies their own particular dream. It is totally ordinary and unavoidable; however, in the event that you cling to the dream too firmly, it can spell trouble for you. Most couples come into a step family suspecting that the family will promptly gel, the relationships will be tight, everybody will feel the adoration, and the family will be a cheerful one. However, it truly does not work that way. In a step family, these dreams set up the potential for significant frustration because since all relatives accompany their own dream, some of which are totally contrary.

Chapter 1: The Toddler—A Curious Little Person

In the caseof behavioral development, we can expect our children to go through four different stages in the early years of their lives. The first stage is from birth until your child reaches 1 year old. This is primarily called the baby stage. Stage 2 goes from 1 to 2½years old called the younger toddler. Stage 3 is from 2½to 4 years old known as the preschool toddler. Finally, stage 4 from 4 years old up to 8 years of age or called the early school-age child. Within this said framework, children grow in size and behavior. Their behavior will change, but not necessarily for the better. This is where parents like you come in.

For toddlers, having the ability to finally do things on their own given their acceleration of freedom, this stage is exciting. For parents, toddlerhood is the perfect time to teach their kids early on of controls and limits. This will be all about learning to control their bodies and behavior.

Some of the following controls include:

Control of behavior – learning that tantrums are not the right way to get parents' attention and influence them

Control of bodily functions – such as being toilet or potty trained

Control over selfishness – learning that toys and food are meant to be shared. Even attention from parents and everything that he thinks belongs to him are to be shared.

Control over frustration – it is like knowing and understanding that their so called "freedom" does not always mean they can do things successfully. Perfect examples are feeding, bathing, and changing clothes.

Control of separation anxiety – moving from close clinginess to be on their own at preschool, and later on, big school.

What Makes Toddlers Tick

Whether you think they are heaven sent, big treasure, terrible 2-year-old, or an explorer, all toddlers have one thing in common. They have these behavioral traits you never dared imagine existed. Some of these traits include:

Toddlers have little to zero sense

Ages 1 to 2 years old, toddlers are considered to have zero sense. It is because, during this time, all they got is maximum mobility and minimum sense. We all know that this combination is psychologically upsetting for parents like you. This is the stage wherein your toddler is unthinking and will just do what he pleases – climbing up and down staircases, scattering toys, eating inedible stuff, and a whole lot more.

Toddlers at this age also get into trouble fighting with their siblings, and they do not know when to stop. Other unthinking behaviors include head-banging, spilling milk on bed sheets, and just simply messing around the whole house. For effective discipline, parents should know when it is best to just slow down or admit defeat. Unfortunately, for some, admitting defeat is impossible thinking that they should be the one in control and in command. While this is true, there will be instances when it is better off to just rest your case.

What is even more frustrating is that there are parents who are making heavy weather of bringing up their children. They often misunderstand these behaviors that they thought their children exist only to annoy them. They slowly forget the fun of having kids around and begin to focus on parenting as an exhausting task and routine.

Toddlers are self-centered

This is a fact; toddlers only focus on their own happiness and needs. They do not have a care in the world simply because they are still young and do not understand what is going on. It is like having a tunnel vision where all they see and care is for their own best and interest.

Sharing of toys or politely asking for it is never going to happen if you have a toddler around. The idea of taking turns is quite foreign at this age as well. And although they love being around other children, they are more focused on being beside kids their age rather than being with them.

For parents, you don't have to worry, this behavior is normal. As the years progress and as your toddler matures, he will surely get through self-centeredness.

Toddlers want constant attention from parents

Most of the time, toddlers love to be the center of attention. If you notice, when your toddler is with another toddler or with a number of kids, the one who steals the limelight will surely be hated. This example does not only extend to playmates but even to simple chores and activities such as cooking, a lengthy phone call, or even when their daddy suddenly hugs or kisses mommy.

Attention is important to toddlers. Since they have little to zero sense, all they think and believe is that mommy or daddy is always there for them. But after a day of messy play, trying to keep the house in order in between plays, and taking care of your toddler's needs, parents are already exhausted. What's more is that you are not just going to do it for 24 hours, but for the rest of your life or as long as they need a Mom and Dad beside them.

The "No" word

Think how many times you have said this word to your toddler. According to experts, toddlers only copy what they hear and see from their parents, and learn to say the word "no" long before they learn to say "yes'.

Toddlers have short attention span

Have a toddler sit on a chair with a toy or food on his hand, and he will last doing the activity only for 3 – 5 minutes. 3 minutes if he finds it interesting and 5 minutes if he begins to be more curious about it. What does this mean? It means that they only live for the here and now. Therefore, it is at this age when constant supervision, guidance, and praises come into play.

And so, if you have a toddler who whines all the time, who demands more stage position, who is self-centered, and has more power than sense, do not fret. You are not the only parent who is going through or has gone through the same situation. Parents, these are all normal behaviors, so there is no need for blaming or for feeling unworthy or not good enough for your children. Just be the best Mom and Dad that you can be, and go with the flow. Who knows, you might learn a thing or two with your terrible 2's.

Chapter 2: How To Smartly Set The Limits

The process of constructing your child's character and creating a favourable version of them entails establishing some boundaries which are expected to provide the basis of correct upbringing. These boundaries should be smartly detected and set, but what is meant by considering boundaries "smart"?

To speak clearly, the child has the right to be set free AND should be confined at some aspects at the same time. Both of these upbringing actions should be simultaneously and equally present, without anyone overweighing the other.

But, how is that possible? What is meant by all of that?

The child is in the need to be set free so as for them to discover themselves; find out about their own talents, passions, potentials, inclinations, powers and interests. If not allowed this room of freedom, the child is expected to experience consistent and persistent oppression, the future outcome of which is almost always not at all favourable.

Simultaneously with granting your child that precious liberty, boundaries are to be set from your end so as for the safety of your child to be warranted.

It is essentially about accompanying your child in their journey of self-discovery, demonstrating your actual presence and support without exaggerated unnecessary interfering acts. By being consistently nearby, you would be able to witness how your child is progressing, and to closely take notice to what could be wrong. You would also be able to recognise the genuine passions and interests of your child, which allows you a chance to get to know your child in a much better way AND get to assist them in developing the passions and talents you discover in them.

When you are nearby, watching your child freely exploring themselves and what they want, you are entitled to and responsible of taking part in the following:

Ensure your child's safety by providing an appropriate environment with appropriate boundaries that allow them a room to roam innocently and freely, to get to know life at its reality, with its different situations and acquaint themselves with them under your supervision and guidance.

Your child is gradually endeavouring to become independent. Do not hurdle this process under any guise or excuse. It is healthier and smarter to implant in your child the core and essences of independence as early as possible, so as for them to grow up accustomed to do vast majority of tasks themselves. You are not supposed to help your child in every single step and task to the extent of rendering them almost totally reliant on you. When you notice your child trying to, for example, return something to its original place, sit on the chair independently, or tidying the surrounding place after playing with toys – praise and motivate them for what they are doing. Keep encouraging them whenever such behaviours are manifested. It is obviously and doubtlessly significant in reinforcing their self-esteem and self-confidence, and also, well, preserving your mental health in the future as you certainly don't wish to have adults who are absolutely reliant on you, even at the simplest of issues to an annoying extent!

You do not have to fix and rectify all the mistakes all the time. Give your children a chance to do so themselves, using their own brains and capabilities. Allow them enough liberty to discover errors and think of solutions with minimal to no interference of yours. This also contributes to formulating an independent self-confident personality that is capable of self-learning and independently analysing and solving problems without relying on you in literally every single conflict, even the simplest of them. In addition, teaching your children to think independently and to detect and solve problems themselves does contribute to elevating their intelligence level, as well as expanding their spectrum of thinking and viewing the world. This can to some extent play a role in establishing an open-minded highly intellectual human being.

Children are expected to be obedient to rules and regulations, as well as to what their parents command and request from them. At the same time, it is quite natural to expect that they would not comply to all your commands and demands literally and blindly. In other words, sometimes your children should experience the mistake so as for them to learn from it and avoid its repetition. Sometimes they have to break the rules (regardless of whether intentionally or the otherwise) so as for them to learn the truth and commit to what is right. You should not expect from your children all the time to actively respond to what you dictate them without having them experience at least some of what you warn them in real life (well, of course there are some things that must NEVER be experienced to be avoided!). You are hence recommended to deal with this matter with patience, flexibility and comprehension. Appreciate and evaluate the overall situation carefully before you hasten to ground or punish your child. Remember that some situations are better to be experienced or at least witnessed (for example, smoking) to introduce the child to what it is like in reality and consequently render them discouraged and unwilling to fall for such inacceptable deeds.

Everything when exceeding limits start to impact in a reverse manner. To speak clearly, you are expect to give love, care and protection to your child. You ought at the same time to realise the limits of these emotions you are supplementing. As too less is unhealthy and dangerous, too much is also so. You must be cautious of transforming your child from a mentally healthy, exuberant, lively and stable individual to someone who is intolerably spoilt, insecure, reliant, and sometimes rude and impulsive. There must be a balance between strictness and leniency, with each of them being implemented in the right situations at the right time, otherwise what appears to you as a good approach to your child might turn out as completely damaging.

Chapter 3: How To Talk To Your Toddler

Everyone talks about their one-year-old in front of them to other parents, their spouse, friends, and anyone else who will listen. Who doesn't recount a day's events to their spouse while they're having dinner, or compare their kids' personalities with other parents at playgroup? Since young children are around their parents all the time, it's nearly impossible to save all child-related chatter for when the child is sleeping or playing. Adults often assume that because a child doesn't talk much or say words very well, they're not taking in what adults are saying. That's wrong. Your baby is listening, and they understand a lot more than you think.

Often, there's a huge difference between expressive language and receptive language at the toddler stage. Toddlers can understand a complex conversation much earlier than most parents believe.

For example, your baby will recognize his or her name by the time they're four and a half months old, so young babies might pay more attention if you mention their name in conversation. By fourteen months, your baby will be a master at reading your social cues. When you're angry, your voice is louder. When you're happy, you tend to speak softly and breathe slower.

No matter what you're saying, your toddler understands the underlying message. If you complain about your child taking off their diaper but think it's cute, your baby hears a voice with a nice tone. If you're angry about it, your child will hear the anger in your tone.

By the time your baby turns one, most of them know around fifty words. They are simple nouns that will refer to people or objects, such as mommy, daddy, dog, and so on and so forth. Within the next several months, they will begin to put the nouns with verbs and begin to understand sentences.

Then, when they are between eighteen to twenty-one months, they will suddenly launch into a stage known as the language explosion. They will learn an average of nine words a day, and they will start to understand how the word order affects the meaning. Once this occurs, your toddler will begin to figure out not just when you're talking about them, but also what you're saying about them. For example, if your toddler hears you complain about how he pulled on the dog's ears, he'll most likely pick up on his name and the word dog, but he'll also understand you believe he did something bad.

So do you need to curtail what you're saying when your toddler is in the room? Yes and no. Toddlers who have parents who talk about them in a tender, loving way enjoy the attention. Your toddler should be included in your conversations when they are in the room. It makes much more sense to be talking with them rather than around them because this helps strengthen their language skills and their interaction skills at the same time.

However, it's important that you keep negative things you say around your toddler to a minimum. If toddlers hear you always say something about them in a negative fashion, such as, "Katie's a bully," then they can carry that around for a long time. Studies have shown that children can learn words or phrases without knowing what they mean, and then piecing that meaning together at a later date. So if a child is always being called a bully, then that child might take that label on as part of their identity once the meaning has been deciphered.

Still, even sensitive parents will make this mistake and talk about their toddler in front of them from time to time. As long as it isn't all the time, you're not doing terrible damage, but you should be careful. If you wouldn't want that thing said about you, then don't say it in front of your child. Toddlers are little people, no matter how small they are, and they are very impressionable.

So how should you be talking to your toddler?

Tips for Addressing Your Toddler Correctly

Connect before directing. Before you direct your toddler on how to do something or what they should be doing, you should be getting down to their eye level and engaging them with some eye contact to get their attention. Teach your toddler how to focus by saying their name and telling them what you want them to do in order to focus on you, such as, "Katie, I need you to look at me," or "Billy,

I need you to listen to me." Offer the same body language when you're listening to your child. Be sure you don't make your eye contact so intense your child perceives you to be controlling rather than connecting with them.

Address your child. Open your request with their name, such as "Helen, please..."

Be brief. You should have a one-sentence rule. The longer you keep talking, the more likely your toddler will forget what it was they were supposed to do. They'll begin to tune you out. So put your directive in the first sentence you say to your child. Too much talking gives your child the impression you're not sure what you want to say, and if she can keep you talking, then she or he can sidetrack you.

Keep it simple. Use one-syllable words and keep your sentences short. Listen to how your toddler communicates with other toddlers and take note of that. When your child looks disinterested or has a glazed look, then you're not being understood.

Ask your toddler to repeat the request. If your child can't repeat it back to you, then your request is too complicated or too long.

Make an offer they can't refuse. You can reason with toddlers, especially if you want to avoid power struggles. Something such as, "Get dressed so you can play," offers a reason for your child to perform the action.

Be positive. Instead of telling your child to, "Stop yelling," say, "We use our inside voice inside."

Begin directives with "I want." Rather than tell your child to get down, tell them, "I want you to get down." Rather than, "Give Terry a turn," say, "I want you to give

Terry a turn now." This works with toddlers who want to please you but don't want to be ordered around. By saying, "I want," you're giving a reason for complying rather than just ordering your toddler to do something.

"When...Then." Say, "When you brush your teeth, then we'll read the story," Or, "When you finish picking up your toys, then we can go outside to play." The word 'when' implies you expect your toddler to listen and obey and works better than the word 'if' because it suggests to your child that they have a choice when you don't intend to.

Actions First, Words Second. Instead of telling your child it's soon time for dinner from the other room, walk into the room where your child is playing and get down to their level. Quietly and firmly tell your child it's almost time for dinner, and then get involved with your child's interest for a few minutes. Going to your toddler tells them you're serious about the request; otherwise, it looks like a preference.

Give them choices. "Do you want to put on your PJs first, or brush your teeth first?" "Do you want the red shirt or the blue shirt?"

Speak to your child according to their development level. The younger your toddler is, the shorter and simpler your requests should be. Consider your toddler's level of understanding. As an example, many parents will ask their three-year-old why they did something. Most adults can't even answer that question, so why expect your three-year-old to answer it? Instead, say something along the lines of, "Let's talk about what just happened."

Speak socially correct to your toddler. Even two-year-olds understand the concept of 'please.' Expect politeness from your toddler. Children shouldn't feel that manners are optional. Speak to your child the way you'd want them to speak to you.

Speak psychologically right. Judgment openers and threats are likely to make your child defensive. 'You' messages will make your child clam-up. 'I' message are not accusing. Rather than saying, "You'd better put your toys away…" or, "You must put your toys away…," try, "I would like it if you…" or, "I'm so happy (or pleased) when you…" Instead of saying, "You need to brush your teeth," say, "I need you to brush your teeth." Don't ask leading questions when negative answers aren't an option. "Will you pick up your toys please?" Just say, "Pick up your toys, please."

Write it down. Reminders easily evolve into nagging, especially for a preteen who might not respond to being told to do something over and over again. Without saying a word, you can communicate everything you have to say. Talk with a paper and pen. Leave a humorous note for a child old enough to read, and sit back and watch what you want being done.

Talk your child down. The louder your child is yelling, then the softer you should be responding. Let your child vent while you interject some soft comments, such as, "I understand," and, "Let me help." Sometimes, just being a caring listener winds down the tantrum your toddler is having. If you come in at their level, you have two tantrums to handle: yours and his or hers.

Settle listeners. Before you tell your toddler to do something, restore emotional balance. Otherwise, you're wasting time. Nothing will sink in when your toddler is an emotional wreck.

Replay the message. Toddlers have to be told to do something a lot. Children who are under two have a hard time remembering your orders. Most three-year-olds will start to internalize your orders so they sink in. Do less and less repeating as your child becomes older. Preteens will regard your repetition as nagging.

Let your toddler complete your thought. Rather than saying, "Don't leave your toys out," try, "Lauren, think of where you'd like to put your toys." Letting your child fill in the blanks can create a lasting lesson.

Use rhyming rules. "If you hit, you sit." Have your child repeat them. It's easier for rhyming rules to sink in.

Give a likable alternative when you can. "You can't go to the park alone, but you can play in the back yard."

Give your toddler advanced notice. "We're going to be leaving soon. Say goodbye to your toys, goodbye to your sister, goodbye to grandpa…"

Open up a closed off toddler. Carefully chosen phrases will open up your toddler's closed off mind and mouth. Stick to topics you know your child will become excited about. Ask a question that requires more than just a yes or a no. Stick to the specifics. Rather than, "Did you have a good day at school," try, "What's the most interesting thing you did today at school?"

"When you…I feel…Because…" "When you run out into the road, Daddy feels scared because you could get hit."

End the discussion. If matters are really closed to discussing them, then say so. "I'm not going to change my mind about this. I'm sorry." You'll save a lot of time, as well as wear and tear on both you and your child. However, reserve this for only when you really mean it.

Specific Examples

Let's look at a few specific examples to give you some more ideas about how to handle a situation with your toddler.

You're feeling really frustrated right now.

When you realize your toddler's about to have a tantrum, you can often get them to calm down and listen by kneeling down, looking into their eyes, and labeling their emotions for them. When you say, "That made you upset," you'll help him or her understand it's normal to experience strong and sometimes frightening emotions. Your words help them process the emotions they're feeling, and when they're a little older, they'll be able to say, "I'm upset," or, "I'm really happy," all by themselves.

Stop, that's hot.

If you want to make a point about something being dangerous, then keep it short and simple. Use only three to four words. Parents will over-explain a situation and the meaning gets lost in all those words. It's okay to use a firm, "No," when you need to get their attention immediately if they're going to hurt themselves or someone else. But if your child constantly hears the word 'no,' then he or she will start to tune it out. If that's already happened, you need to baby-proof your house so your child can explore without always hearing reprimands.

It's time to take a bath now.

Many parents will make the mistake of asking their child if they want to do something, but it's better to use statements when you need your child to transition into another activity, such as taking a bath. When you inquire about something, you are giving your child a choice, which opens up the normal routine to being a conflict. The rule you need to follow is not to ask, just tell when there isn't really an option.

First...Then...

Your toddler has some foggy notions about time, so when you tell your toddler you're going to do something in fifteen minutes, it doesn't mean much to them. Rather than giving them a time frame, describe the sequence of events. For example, "First we're going to clean up, and then we're going to get dressed, so we're ready to go."

Do your socks go on first, or do your pants go on first?

Let your child make the simpler choices as part of their daily routine. When you hand over just a tad bit of control, you're boosting their confidence when they get to do something. However, a choice between just two items is enough. Younger kids have limited memory and attention spans, and they just can't keep track of everything.

You're throwing food; all done.

To manage a toddler's behavior at the table, you need to act quickly and use the same short phrases every time. If your toddler has a tendency to throw food, then use a simple phrase like the one listed above. Keep a calm tone, and then remove your toddler from the table to get them away from the situation.

I like how you held my hand when we were in the busy store.

Positive reinforcement, pointing out what they did right, is a strong motivator for them. Even if they don't completely understand, your toddler will pick up on the rhythm and the cadence with which you say the words, and they will understand some of the meaning.

Let's name the animals in the book.

You're most likely teaching your toddler to name simple things, such as body parts, colors, and foods, but finding more subjects to talk about with them helps them make new language connections. Remember, they can learn a lot of words in just one day. Point out different objects in the books you read to them every time you read the book together. While you're in the park, use descriptive words. Instead of saying, "Look at that tree," say, "Look at that tall tree with red leaves." This helps them see the world in a new way.

Some of the important takeaways you should remember from this chapter are:

Do not use baby talk with your toddler. They are learning a lot of information on a daily basis, and speaking to them in an adult manner teaches them how to socialize and interact on a higher level.

Never give your toddler a choice when there isn't really a choice, and keep choices down to just two. Your toddler only has so many reasoning skills right now, and giving them a choice when there isn't one is just unfair.

Your toddler is amazing and can understand the words you're saying around them, even if they're not forming those words into sentences themselves yet. Watch what you're saying around them.

Chapter 4: Hitting, Kicking, And Biting

Toddlers are amazing little people. They are becoming aware that they are separate people from their parents and that they are individuals; they are learning that they can assert themselves. They want independence, and they want everyone to know what they like as well as what they dislike.

While all of this is going on, toddlers also have very limited self-control and are just starting to learn how to share, take turns, and wait for their needs to be met. While it is an exciting time for them, it can also be confusing and terrifying as well.

Here is a common example of toddler behavior.

Max is quietly playing with his toy truck when Jon yanks it out of his hand and starts playing with it. Max watches quietly for a few seconds as Jon pushes the truck around, thinking about how he can get it back. Quickly he jumps up and heads toward Jon, but Jon sees him coming and grips the truck as he stands up trying to protect it. Max quickly shoves Jon forcing him to fall back and to let go of the truck before he snatches up his truck and heads back to his play area.

Max sits down with his truck just as Jon begins to stand up. Max watches as Jon begins walking toward him. Max wraps his arms around his truck this time and begins yelling, "Mine! My truck."

Both Max's and Jon's parents have been watching the entire situation unfold and quickly walk over to the two boys. For what seems like the thousandth time, the parents tell the boys to use their words and not their hands in a calm voice before walking away. Max glares at Jon as he clutches the truck and before the parents know it, the boys are back at it again.

One thing that we as parents have to remember is that toddlers are just learning how to communicate and while we may ask them regularly to use their words or tell us what they want, they may not be able to do so all of the time.

You see, while a child may be able to take you by the hand and show you what it is that they want off of a shelf by pointing at it, the same is not true when it comes to expressing their anger. This is when biting, hitting, kicking, pushing, and other aggressive behaviors begin to be displayed.

When toddlers are aggressive, they are trying to communicate something to you.

For example, "I want to be alone," "You are too close," "I want that toy," "I am bored," "I am tired," and so on.

Just like any other area of development when it comes to aggressive behavior, there is a wide range that can be displayed. Some children will rarely display aggressive behavior, and when they do, it will not be very aggressive at all. Other children may display highly aggressive behavior a lot of the time, and this often concerns parents. The good news when it comes to this type of aggressive behavior is that between the ages of 18 months and 3 years, it is perfectly normal. That is as long as you see a decrease in aggressive behavior as the child matures.

Aggressive behavior, however, can become worrisome when the child grows older and becomes very aggressive. This can signal that there are some developmental issues going on, and it should be looked into by a doctor.

It is also important to understand that children who generally overreact to a situation are going to be more prone to aggressive behavior. Another thing that causes children to behave aggressively is that they see this behavior displayed by the adults in their life.

I want to spend a few minutes talking about imitating the behavior that they see at home before we move on to normal aggressive behavior and how to handle it.

If a child is raised in a home where hitting is seen as okay when the child makes the parent mad, the child is going to think that when someone else makes them mad, it is okay to become physical and hit them. You absolutely cannot expect a toddler to understand that there is a difference between you spanking them and them hitting another child. Not only do spanking and hitting create aggressive toddlers but homes, where yelling is the norm, do so as well.

These toddlers see their parents out of control. They see adults that have no idea how to control their own emotions, and they learn very quickly that this is how they are supposed to behave. If you are having a hard time controlling your emotion, then it is important that you spend time workings on this before you ever try to work on your toddler's aggression.

As the parent of a toddler, it is your job to teach your child how to not only understand but also control their emotions. You have to begin teaching the child how they can communicate their needs and their wants not only to you but also to those around them without becoming aggressive. This, of course, like most of the parenting, is not an easy task, and it is going to take a lot of patience and time. However, it is possible.

When you are dealing with an aggressive toddler, you have to understand first that no two children are alike. While you may not have had to deal with aggression from your first born, your second child may be very aggressive. This is not because you did anything differently while taking care of the two children. You did not provide one child with more attention than the other, and one does not feel more loved than the other. This is simply because the two are different children with different personalities and deal with their emotions in different ways.

In order to understand this aggression that your child is displaying, you need to ask yourself what types of situations usually cause your child to display aggressive behavior. See if there are certain times of the day, if there are certain situations or if there are similar situations that cause your child to act aggressively.

The next thing you need to do is ask yourself why you think this is happening. Why do you think that your child is acting aggressively in each situation? Are you planning play dates right before nap time? Does your child simply not understand how to share their toys? Is your child getting upset because he or she does not know how to communicate what they want?

What do you do when your child acts aggressively? I hate to see parents brag about how they smacked their child in the mouth because he or she bit another child. This is not how we should be teaching our children to control their emotions. Are you acting aggressively when your child does? Are you returning hit for a hit? Do you really take the time to try and understand what it is that is upsetting your child or are you too wrapped up in your own feelings and embarrassment?

Is the way that you are reacting to your child's aggressive behavior beneficial to the child or is it doing more harm than good? Why do you feel this way? If you have to, take out a notebook and start jotting these answers down. It will give you something good to think about later when you are getting ready for bed or while the family watches television.

If you do not feel that your reactions are benefiting your child, how can you change that? How do you think you should be reacting to your child's behavior and what can you do to ensure that you react differently next time?

It is also important to understand what type of behavior to expect from what age.

From birth up to the age of one year, parents need to understand that babies have little control over their movements, and they explore the world by biting and putting things in their mouth. Many times, parents can feel rejected when a baby grabs hold of their hair and pulls or pinches their nose and will not let go. We get upset when they swat a spoon out of our hands when all we are trying to do is feed them, but the truth is no baby is purposely trying to hurt your feelings. They do not even understand that you have feelings. They are just trying to learn about the world and explore it in the only way that they know.

From one to two years of age is when aggression usually peaks. This is when the child will hit and kick the parent, bite kids, swat you on purpose and mean to cause pain when they pull your hair. This is when a toddler is experiencing very strong emotions.However, they are not able to express them through their words. Think about this story: Max is sitting on the living room floor contently playing with his mom's cell phone. He loves pushing all of the buttons, pulling up pictures and even taking a few of his own. When mom walks into the living room and sees Max playing with her phone, she quickly takes it out of his hand telling him that it is not a toy.

Max jumps up and kicks his mom right in the leg. She reaches down to pick him up only to get kicked again.

Max cannot tell his mother that he was having fun with the cell phone. He does not understand that it costs money or what money even is. All he knows is that he was happy playing with it, not bothering anyone, and suddenly, she took it away. Max uses his aggression to show his mother that he is not pleased that she took the phone and that he wants it back.

Instead of getting upset with Max and making a big deal out of the aggressive behavior, it is better if the mother gives Max something else to play with and puts her phone in an area where he cannot get to it.

From the age of two to three, aggression is usually displayed when a toddler is feeling overwhelmed with the situation, they are distressed or even jealous. This is often displayed as the child begins preschool. While the toddler cries that they do not want their parent to leave, they may hit the parent, shove a friend away that is trying to comfort them or hit the teacher.

This is the age when it is time to start setting rules, but it is also not the time to be extremely stern to a child. When a child is distressed, they need to know that they are going to be okay, that the adult understands they are upset, but they also need to be reminded that hitting is not okay.

It is also important for parents to understand that toddlers of this age are still unable to control their impulses. While they may know that the rule says they are not allowed to hit, they do not know how to stop themselves from hitting when they get the urge. Their emotions are going to be in control at least for now.

When a toddler displays aggressive behavior, it is because he or she is out of control or overwhelmed. It is not the time to begin teaching the child, but the time to recognize what is going on and help the child through the situation. When the child has moved past the aggression, you can then talk to them about it, but you should never expect a toddler to be able to control their emotions.

What can you do?

The first thing that you must do when your child is displaying aggressive behavior is to start paying attention to the details. Make a note of where the behavior is taking place. Is it happening at home? At preschool? At daycare? Does it happen everywhere?

If you find that this behavior is happening in one specific place, you need to start asking what could be causing this behavior. It could be that the specific area is too crowded or that it overwhelms the child causing them to display aggressive behavior.

Ask yourself if the behavior is directed at one specific person. If the behavior is directed at one person, it could be that the child simply does not feel comfortable around that person or does not like that person.

When does the behavior happen? Is there a certain time of day when you see these types of behavior? For example, does the toddler become aggressive right before nap time or maybe when the child is transitioning from one activity to another or when the child is hungry? A child facing these types of stressors often displays aggressive behavior because they do not know how to deal with the stress in any other way.

What was going on right before the child displayed aggressive behavior? You may find that the child has a hard time dealing with situations such as leaving the park, or you might find that the child is aggressive when another child takes a toy out of their hand. It is important to know what is setting the child off so that you can help the child learn how to handle these situations.

Ask yourself, if there have been any changes to the child's life. Many parents are surprised when they realize something small can set off aggressive behavior, such as switching rooms in daycare. Other times it can be much bigger events, such as a divorce, moving or a new sibling being added to the family. This can make the child feel insecure, and they have no idea how to deal with this insecurity so they often become aggressive.

Many people like to stick their noses in the air and look down on the parent of a child that is aggressive, but it is important for you to understand as that parent that your child's aggressive behavior is normal. It simply means that your child is developing normally, and while it can be upsetting at times, it is up to you to be patient with the child as they learn how to explore the world around them. It is up to you to teach the child what is acceptable and what is not acceptable without disciplining them for something that comes naturally to them.

Chapter 5: Raising A Creative Child

An American actor, director, screenwriter, and author named Alan Alda says, "The creative is the place where no one else has ever been. You have to leave the city of your comfort and go into the wilderness of your intuition. What you'll discover will be wonderful. What you'll discover is yourself."

Creativity can help your child become a better person. Home is where the child discovers his abilities for the first time whereas he also realizes his creative self. Therefore it is wrong to assume that creativity is something children are naturally born with. The truth is creativity is just like confidence; it's not an inborn talent but rather a skill that needs improvement. As a parent, you can help your child discover his creative mind.

Here are some ways to reveal your child's creativity:

Provide tools and resources your child needs to express his creativity. Give him the time he needs to express his imagination and feelings. Provide him space where he can do creative activities. It is a place where he is free to make a mess. Then give him materials such as art supplies or building materials that he can manage to work on.

Make your home open for discussion. For instance, during dinnertime, you may talk about different creative activities to encourage your child to think of things that he has not done before. Don't choose the best for him; allow him to decide for himself.

Allow him to commit mistakes. If he fails, encourage him to spot his mistake, learn from it and correct it. It will help if you share with him your personal mistakes and how you dealt with them.

Allow your child to explore his ideas and do what he wants. Don't boss him around. Putting limits on what he does can only develop his fear for failure and may affect his self-esteem.

Give your child the freedom to express "opposing thoughts". Let him disagree with your ideas. Encourage him to find more than one solution to a problem. Let him explore different ways to create something.

Don't motivate your child with rewards or incentives. Don't give him something in return for expressing creativity. This act will only interfere with his interests, thus reducing the quality of his creativeness.

Don't focus on what your child can achieve. Look more intently on the process rather than the result. Make sure he had fun doing the activity. Allow him to determine what he likes about the activity.

As a parent, you want to help your child as much as you can. But don't get too caught up with it that you start pushing your child around. Let him enjoy the activity that he loves doing without the pressure of being nagged. Allow him to have fun. Be open to playfulness and getting messy.

Chapter 6: Responsibilities Of An Adult

As a child there are certain things that you can get away with. We let things go as parents and use lines like 'boys will be boys', 'girls just want to have fun', or some other variation. But to prepare your child for the big wide world you need to impress upon them the weight of responsibility. They might still be your baby, but in the eyes of their peers and the rest of the world they are now an adult. So they had better act like one to avoid the very adult consequences that they may face if they fail to act correctly.

Lesson #6: Good manners

The old saying goes, "A little courtesy goes a long way". In the past there were etiquette schools that children could attend to learn the correct ways to act in various situations. These days such schools have mostly faded out of existence and so it is up to us as parents to impart such wisdom to our children. It is important to teach your kids the importance of saying thank you when something good happens to them, or a please when they are inquiring for something, otherwise they may come off as rude and impolite.

Suggested Mannerisms to focus on

You no doubt have been working to instill many of these throughout your children's life to date. However it does not hurt to bring these things to the forefront of their minds once again before you release them out into the world away from your watchful and encouraging eye.

Saying polite words such as 'Please', 'Thank you', 'You're welcome', or 'Excuse me'

Look someone in the eye when you are talking to them

How to politely shake someone's hand (firm grip, but not hard - very important for job interviewing)

Not to say negative things about other people behind their back

Table manners such as no elbows on the table and chewing with their mouth closed

I personally try to bring these points and others up with my children every time I notice them or someone else doing something out of line. I find that it makes a very big difference on a child's psyche if they see you as a parent actually pointing out and commenting on others behavior and manners. It can make them more aware that the world is judging them as you as a parent have said that it will. Focusing on family, friends, characters in movies and TV shows have all worked well to prove such points in the past for me.

Key Takeaways

By instilling polite manners in your child you are teaching them to have respect for themselves and respect for others. Being polite and having good manners will help your child to make a good impression when meeting new people in school, work, and their social life. The positive reaction that this can cause can help to build confidence and identity when they are out on their own. It can also help them avoid unnecessary conflicts that result from rudeness.

This may seem unnecessary to reinforce before your child goes out on their own, and they will no doubt see it as you babying them, but it is important. It gives you an added measure of confidence in them and can let you rest easier knowing that you have given them all of the help and encouragement that you could while they were at home. Your child may one day thank you for these lessons when they impress a partners parents or their new boss at a dinner or event by being polite and having the correct manners.

Lesson #7: How to choose the right friends

"You are judged by the company you keep" is something that my mother always said to me. Surrounding oneself with positive or negative friends can have a huge impact on your outlook on life and your attitude. What friends are doing can be very influential in determining the kind of life decisions that your teen will make. Being surrounded by the wrong friends can lead to regrettable decisions while good friends can push your teen towards making the right calls on important life decisions.

How to determine a positive friend

As parents we are not blind to the goings on of our children and their friends. You will most likely know who the good apples are and who the bad are already.

Good friends

A positive outlook and enthusiasm for life

They are honest and trustworthy

They are will to help if you need a hand

They are smart and eager to learn

Having a good friend who is trustworthy and loyal can help them get emotional or any other support when they need it. A good friend can also push them to making important life decisions, as well as bring out the best in them.

Bad friends

Looking to take advantage of your child in some way

Deceitful and quick to lie to protect themselves

Overly destructive in their habits - prone to drink too much, try drugs, or fight

Key Takeaways

Again as a parent you will have a very good idea as to which friends are good or bad for your children. Sometimes having a quiet word to your child to voice disapproval of spending time with a friend can be a good idea. I have personally done so with both of my children with regard to a handful of their friends.

Every time I have tried this I have been met with a different response. Sometimes they are open to listening, sometimes they take offense and want to fight me on the subject. There is no magic bullet that can solve every situation. You just need to make it clear to your child that they are judged by the company that they keep and that you disapprove of some of their choices. Time will be the judge of whether your advice gets through, and also whether it was the correct advice or not.

Lesson #8: Observing the Law

I have no doubt that both you and your teen are aware of how the law dictates that your child act. Every country is different in its rules, regulations, and the severity of punishments dictated. If you live in America then the legal drinking age for example is 21 years of age, if you are in Canada it is 19, and in Australia and NZ it is 18. Being ignorant of the law can cause serious repercussions. Before leaving home your child should be aware of general rules and regulations in your area and country. It could help to avoid the unpleasant experience of being arrested and having to call you to bail them out of prison.

Suggested conversations regarding the law

1. Drinking

It is totally understandable that you child will have experiences that involve drinking when they leave home. However, if they are under age or have friends that are, it is important that the drinking is contained to private residences as opposed to public places or bars.

It is also important to point out that drunk and disorderly behavior is not acceptable and that knowing their limit and taking care of their friends when drinking is of the upmost importance.

2. Behavior

Fighting, vandalism, and burglary are all things that we as parents would never expect from our children. However peer pressure can lead to all kinds of undesirable actions once your child leaves home. It is important to remind your child that such actions are not just frowned upon by you as a parent, but that they can actually wind up facing criminal charges because of it. Smart choices are essential when leaving home, and how your child behaves with their new found independence can affect the rest of their life.

3. Driving

Traffic laws and vehicle registration laws need to be upheld at all times. Drinking and driving, speeding, and erratic behavior behind the wheel can not only lead to losing their license, but more importantly it can be fatal. Teenagers believe that they are bulletproof at times, so a friendly reminder that their driving could get them or someone else killed can help to enforce why laws and rules exist in the first place.

4. Online Behavior

Your children may be more informed than you in this area, but it is important to enforce the idea that piracy, and things like online bullying are crimes. If caught performing illegal activities online at school, work, or even at home can lead to expulsion or dismissal. This is not something to be taken lightly.

Key Takeaways

Being made aware of basic laws once again could help your child to avoid breaking them. Some laws and regulations come with heavy fines and jail terms. If they know these laws and what the consequences for breaking them are, they can escape potential fines, jail terms, and more importantly causing themselves or others any harm.

You may feel like a broken record having to repeat these conversations. But if you are like me, you will feel much more secure in the knowledge that your child will act responsibly after hearing your points. Adding your disapproval to the other potential penalties that your child will face if they were to break the law can stop them from making foolish decisions once they leave home.

Chapter 7: Meaning Of Long-Distance Parenting

Distance Parenting is a term that is used to describe the action of parents towards their child or children from a distance in order to fulfill parental obligation towards the kids. It is in the other hand, parent trying to rear and control the child by remote control means from afar to fulfill the act of parenting.

In fact, for so many reasons such as economic, political and social, the phenomenon of Distance Parenting has embedded its self in our societies today. Parents could leave their loved ones behind in a far, far location from where they currently reside. Therefore, the parents now try to control the situation by every possible means so that the physical absence wouldn't cause too much damage in relating with their children.

This sort of control allows the parent, who is not around the children most of the time, to kind of contribute in the physical, social, emotional, intellectual and psychological development of the kids. In fact, circumstance has made it inevitable for some parents, to leave their kids under the care of someone else or relatives. In such a case, the mother or father, even both parents of the kids would endeavor to stay close to the children from afar by frequently communicating with them.

Technically, "Long-Distance Parenting," is practiced by almost every parent, knowingly or unknowingly. For instance, when any parent calls home from the office or elsewhere to inquire from the baby-sitter how the children are doing, that is distance parenting in action. Parents do that from any location or distance, just to monitor the affairs of the kids from a remote place. Therefore, whenever you call to talk to any person in the house, make sure all grounds are covered, that is to say, the children should be asked about one after the other.

Currently, parents can care for their children from a distance without much frustration, thanks to the Internet and generation of modern Information Technology. Fundamentally, the Information Technology and the Internet have made distance parenting much more appealing. For obvious reason, gone are those days, months and years of snail-mails and telegrams when parents would leave their children behind and took a trip, only to return and met an awful and ruin family. Typically, my family has been in the art of distance parenting for some times now. In fact, there would be a time in our lives that we got to do what would be the best for the family and distance parenting would become unavoidable and must have to be introduced.

All those periods, the children were looked after by paid relatives or helpers from outside the family while the kids remain in check from a distance. Parents could monitor the welfare of their children from any geographical distance without much frustration anymore, thanks to the technological innovations of the 21st century.

Subsequently, one of the parents would be a bit far from home, leaving the daily care of the children in the hands of one of the parents which is a better ideal, or a helper from outside. Due to the fact that parents go questing for economic or financial freedom for the family, that more often than not results in a vacuum in closer parenting of a child by the biological parents.

Consequently, in this modern time, parents' interactions with their kids happen always during weekends or holidays only. This is because the kids have to be sleeping by the time they get home at night. Most of the time, the natural bonding between parents and the children of the family would start to diminish due to lack of frequent interaction.

However, the telephone and other modern day communication gadgets have made distance parenting less stressful. Specifically, computer and the Internet have covered that vacuum which used to exist in distance parenting and now parents can communicate, interact with their loved ones daily if need be through Skype. The parents can even install a CCTV (Closed-Circuit Television) device in their homes in order to monitor the kids' activities around the house while away from home.

Chapter 8: Simple Ways To Boost Self-Esteem

Self-esteem for kids in their middle years are affected by a variety of different factors. It includes peer pressure, environment, media, and experiences but mostly it is dependent on their parents' actions and words. So while teachers have a role to play, the responsibility of cultivating self-esteem on your daughter lies mostly on your shoulders.

To help you raise a daughter to live a life with high self-esteem, here are some simple ways to do it.

1. Feed her positivity

In a world full of negativity, the only way to win is to be positive. To save your kid from serious side effects of low self-esteem, you have to focus on her strengths and teach her to do the same. Honing optimism at a young age is a great way to set her up for success in the future.

2. Tell her she's beautiful

With media feeding young girls wrong notions of beauty, it's up to you to tell her and make her understand that she's beautiful no matter her size, shape, height, skin color and other physical attributes. While she may not fully grasp the concept yet, it's important to nurture a healthy body image in your child as early as you can.

3. Limit media and internet access

A great deal of what's shown on TV, magazines and the internet portrays a set of unrealistic standards on physical beauty. Do not let these materials shape your daughter's sense of self and beauty. To do that, you have to set limitations on internet use and media exposure. At the same time, you have to build combat the negativity with praises and positive criticism.

4. Be affectionate

The preteen years especially from age 6 to 9 are the ideal times to be more affectionate to your daughter. Time will come when they'd want space and distance from you. Until then, be sure to be generous with your affection. Give her a hug every chance you get, a kiss on the check when she comes from school and tell her you love her all the time.

5. Ask about her day

Meeting new friends and going to school are among the top highlights of a girl in her middle years. To keep the connection bet you and your daughter and keep tab at her activities at the same time, make it a habit to ask her about her day. Give her the chance to talk as most girls love that and listen well while you're at it. When she knows you're genuinely interested, the sharing will become so natural between parent and daughter thereby keeping the relationship healthy and open.

6. Pay attention to her words

To ensure that your daughter develops a high self-esteem, it is important to pay attention to her words. When she says she's not beautiful, not good enough and other negative things of the same variety, you should do something. Oftentimes, there are underlying issues masked in those words and talking to her about it is one way to get to the bottom of the problem.

7. Watch your words

If you don't want her talking about herself negatively, you shouldn't talk in the same manner as well. Parents, after all, are the top people young girls look up to as their role model. If you watch your words, she will do the same because you set the right example for her. This means no calling her names or labeling her as this and that out of anger.

8. Adjust when necessary

No girls in their middle years are exactly the same way which means there is also no absolute parenting style that's right for everyone. As you daughter navigates the preteen years, you have to be prepared to adjust your parenting style whenever needed. Just because your friend's daughter is like an angel doesn't mean you should expect yours to be the same way.

9. Be consistent with discipline

Discipline is essential at any age of a child's development. If you want to develop self control, set proper expectations and ensure a healthy environment for growing up, you need to set limits and enforce disciplinary measures when necessary. To control behavior, you can establish house rules like no name calling or no negative talking. When the rules are broken, appropriate punishment should be enforced.

10. Make time for her

More than the discipline and other child-rearing to do's, making time for her is probably the most important part of raising a confident child. Kids aged 6 to 9 still love spending time with family. As a good parent, it's a must to prioritize quality time with your daughter. No matter how busy you are, if you make time for her, she'll know that she is valued and loved boosting her sense of self worth in the process.

Chapter 9: Self-Development For A Modern Kid

Do you know that this era, more than any other era in human history, has been the one with the most children millionaires and adults past the age of 50 still making an impact on society and developing themselves daily? You cannot help but notice that it is everywhere now. Information. It is the very fabric of life we live now; there is so much data flying around these days that it is absolutely impossible not to learn something new every day if you are on the internet or watching the television for news or other media content. Even television shows are tailored towards helping people learn more about the world these days.

I cannot even begin to tell you how much of the things that people use today were made or innovated by youths. The world today is revolving and so many things are changing faster than most people can say YouTube. (Okay, maybe that was a bit of a stretch). However, the kinds of changes going on in the world today due to technology and innovation have forced the classroom to be barely adequate rather than being an absolute for a child to be useful in this era. This is not to say education in a classroom is not necessary; after all, it is still one of the few ways in which most kids get to socialize physically with people these days. However, you should take the time out to teach your kids one or two things that are necessary for them to survive in the future and be a self-sustaining adult, as well as a contributing member in the society.

Some self-development techniques you should use on your kids

There are so many ways to make sure that your kids are getting the right kind of education, so I am going to list a few here that are essential.

Be a good role model

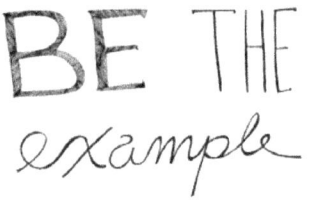

One of the best ways to teach our kids what we want them to do is by doing those things ourselves. Our kids grow up with the notion that what their parents do is usually the right things since the parents are usually the first-hand examples that

they have on how to do many of the things they do in life. Therefore, it is the obligation of you as a parent to make sure that you always model the kind of character you would like to see in your kids.

Like Rick Rigsby, retired professional athlete, entrepreneur and motivational speaker once said,

"My dad's job required him to resume by 7 am but he woke up every day at 4:3o am and he would be at the office by 6 am before anybody else. One day, his mum asked his dad why he always got up at the same time for over 15 years, and his dad replied saying, I do because I hope that one day, one of my kids would wake up and catch me in an act of excellence."

Rick Rigsby has never been known to attend any conference or meeting later than anyone in the meeting. He is usually the first to arrive and he gives all the credit to his father.

You too can try to display attitudes and character traits that you would like to see in your kids. This is the best way to make sure that they will develop into the model citizens that they want you to be.

Teach them the importance of values

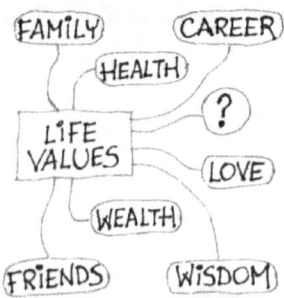

When your child is still young and under your wings, this is the right time to start to teach him/her, right and wrong, good and bad in the clearest possible terms, because in the end life has never been black and white. You should actively teach your kids what your values are, like showing respect to their elders, being kind to the next person, show love and care to those in need and also to never let anyone treat them like they are inferior. You have to start teaching your kids from an early age how to be confident in themselves. This will let them go very far in life and also help them face adversities when they do come. One of the best ways to do this is by telling them stories that show the importance of these values, show them real-life examples of people that display these values in their lifestyle and you should let them read the book either on or offline about the importance of the values that you have taught them.

A good example of a child with the right values is that of Rachel Beckwith. She had heard about how it was hard for people in poor African villages to get clean water and on her birthday, she made a wish to raise $300,o00 in fundraising in order to kick-start a fundraising campaign that would help Charitywater.org bring clean water to these kinds of villages. It turned out when she was just $80 short of her goal, she died three days after being in a multi-vehicle crash. The news of her wish got around to people around the world and in her honor, they helped her raise over a million dollars for the cause which she believed in. She might be deceased now, but for a child that lived a life so short, she made an impact so big due to the kind of values her parents had imbibed in her or maybe she was just a cool kid, who knows, right!

Always make your kids learn

Of course, we all know how important learning can be in the life of a child. But in this age, learning for a child is not what it used to be a couple years back. Now there are so many ways in which your kids can learn. This is mostly due to technological advancements, of course. You should learn to use this to your advantage; ask your kids what they feel passionate about and encourage them to do it. If it involves going to a boot camp, a workshop or a seminar to enable them to kickstart their dreams, then you should make sure you do it for them if feasible. Some of them only require a few books, an internet connection, and a superfast computer to make their dreams come alive. If this is in your capacity then you should do it and if not, you should find ways in which you can empower your kids to do what they love. Trust me, it will be worth it in the end. The value of making sure that your kids are in touch with the right resources that would enable them to carve their own path in this world is invaluable. These days, we hear so much of teenage entrepreneurs and young millionaires in their twenties that had just an ambition and a few resources to work with. Your kids might just be some of the next ones.

A good example is the story of Ninja, a professional game streamer who is only 27 years old. In 2018, Ninja had more social media interactions than Lebron James, Cristiano Ronaldo, and Shaquille O'Neal, which made him the most popular athlete in the world. He earns over $500,000 per month from playing video games online at a professional level.

Also, there is the story of 6-year-old, Ryan who makes over $14 million dollars in a year just by reviewing toys on YouTube. All because his parents let him do what he loved on camera.

This is not to say YouTube is the only place your child can make it, but you should, however, understand that social media and the internet is likely going to be a necessary tool for your child to grow his/her passion.

For instance, at the age of 13, Rachel Zietz became the CEO to her own company, which is a largely successful online sportswear company, Gladiator Lacrosse. She became a self-made millionaire by 15. She is a Lacrosse player herself and this is where her passion for making attire for the sport came from. She made over $2 million dollars in 2018, while studying economics at Princeton University.

So, you see as a parent, all you have to do is let the creative part of your child shine, and if you have more than one child, you should remember that all children are different and the passion of A may most likely be different from that of B. Therefore, learn to study them, talk to them and determine what the best learning experience for them would be.

Chapter 10: Peaceful, Patient, And Positive Parenting

In certain situations, maintaining calmness, patience, and perseverance can be very difficult. However, it is possible. The only thing that gets in the way is how you, as a parent, look at your child's unpleasant behavior.

Children are small figures in an adult's world. Each of them is born with their own temperament and their right to choose what to do, whether it is useful or harmful to them. Since children speak in "other" languages, it is sometimes difficult for parents to understand them. From the parents' point of view, their little ones are too immature to make any decisions at all. However, it is true that, regardless of the consequences, children have the right to choose what they will do at certain times. You must be patient through this process. And that is not easy.

It's hard, but necessary to maintain calmness. If a parent thinks the child is "unresponsive" and that they "can't take the child's behavior anymore," then it is entirely normal for them to lose their patience, and in a large number of cases, lose control as well. Many parents then shout at the child in order to change the child's behavior.

Typical sentences spoken by parents are: "His behavior is so annoying!" Or "She can't learn anything" or "I really don't know what I'm going to do with him". Of course, they are desperate. And wrong. They have tried everything, and nothing helps, so they give up.

A common feature that occurs in these cases is: Parents have lost their patience and lost their persistence.

However, if you step away from this unpleasant situation which makes you feel angry at your child, and you look at it objectively, you won't see the child's perspective as "insignificant" or see him as "misunderstood" but will see that he needs something. From this perspective, you can use logic and try to find out exactly what your child needs and what you need to do to help him. So, as you do this you are constantly and patiently "reading" your child.

So, what is patience?

Being a persistent and patient parent means putting in consistent and constant work to develop quality and constructive communication with your child, because you must reach your child's inner self and feelings. One of the positive side effects that you will achieve as an efficient parent is that, with all of your patience and understanding as you manage the child's behavior and help them, one day, your toddler becomes an emotional intelligent and responsible person.

The essence of positive discipline is to learn to change yourself instead of trying to change others and to make others want to change. If you're busy trying to control your child, you are not thinking about the ability to solve problems by controlling your behavior and making decisions about your actions, rather than trying to correct your child's behavior.

It is easy to fall into the temptation to repeat what you have said, to remind the child of something, and to explain it instead of just doing what you have already said. Careful and resolute parenting gives parents the opportunity to spend time developing the great features that their child possesses, talks with them on many interesting topics, and giving them an explanation of how things work in life.

Punishment: Toughness through love. Should I punish a child?

Apparently, most parents think you should punish a child. But it is important to define the concept of "punishment." Punishment can be a strict tone in your voice, temporarily depriving the child of positive interaction, sweets or any privileges that are reserved for obedient children.

We don't even contemplate using physical punishment, and when parents have outdated ideas about the admissibility of corporal punishment, we hope that they can be immediately corrected!

Of course, it's hard to imagine a mother who has never raised her voice in her life. But we can imagine the surprise of an angry mother, when in response to a slap her own child turns around and does the same thing!

If you punish children physically, you risk making them angry, and depending on the individual characteristics of their personality, they will not only remember everything in detail but may also want to get revenge!

Sometimes the same can be said about moral punishment as well. But of course, if a child who is three years old or older has behaved poorly, knowing in advance that what he did was bad, he should be made aware that it was not right.

Imagine a situation where the child doesn't think about the consequences of his actions or forgets what you have told him earlier. Even if the child did something deliberately disobedient, do not lower yourself to his level and respond in kind. Be patient and be wiser.

Punishments don't help much

If we take into account that the punishment causes a negative emotional state and causes the child to feel embarrassed, frightened, and insecure, we can understand that punishment does not motivate the child to learn from the situation. That is why it is useful for parents to make a decision about what their parenting goal is: absolute obedience or a relationship of trust.

What punishment can do

Punishment implies a loss of opportunity for experiential learning, but also causes a loss of opportunity to create a relationship of trust between you and your child. If the child fears punishment, he will not feel encouraged to learn, to draw conclusions, and later to develop responsibility.

Chapter 11: Single Mom With Toddlers - Handling Temper Tantrums

After your baby has grown up to be a vibrant toddler, and just when you thought your baby has outgrown the irritating bouts of non-stop crying and flailing limbs to catch your attention, comes now the temper tantrums. This time around, it is a more serious, albeit, more violent behavioral problem you will have to face.

It can be as mild as continuous crying and whining with no signs of stopping. Or, it can be more violent and involve ear-shattering screams, breath holding, kicking, and hitting at people or objects. Not all toddlers have it of course but most of them do. And, unless your toddler is one of the rare exceptions, you better understand why toddlers have them so you'd know what to do.

Temper Tantrums and Why Kids Have Them

Temper tantrums are common among 1 to 3 year old toddlers. It is actually part of their normal development so there is no need to push the panic button. Some toddlers manifest temper tantrums on a regular basis while others rarely do. At any rate you should not view toddler temper tantrums negatively.

They are simply manifestations of their frustration in not being able to get a thing or in most cases, their parents to do something they want. And because they don't have the same inhibitions or control of an adult, they vent their frustrations with varying degrees of temper tantrums.

Basically, tantrums are the toddlers' desperate way of communicating a message across to you - like telling you they are tired, or hungry, or uncomfortable with something, or they just want your undivided attention (much like when they were still bottle feeding infants). The only difference is back then, they can only cry and flay their limbs but this time around they know how their bodies work and so they scream, and kick and hit – out of frustration.

Remember they are still learning language and so their ability to communicate is limited. What happens then is the toddlers begin to understand much more than what they are able to express in words. And their inability to communicate what they want leads to frustration which touches off or triggers the tantrums.

As toddlers discover more and more of their surroundings they develop a feeling of independence and a sense of control of everything around them. They begin to think of doing things themselves or wanting the things they fancy and start expecting to be given everything they want. And when they discover the limits to what they can do or find out they can't have everything they want frustration sets in which ultimately precipitates the temper tantrums.

The good news is as the toddler learns to communicate more effectively, and as he develops a better understanding of the things around him, his level of frustration diminishes and ultimately just fades away.

So, how should you deal with your toddler's temper tantrums?

Will you hit or spank the child? Absolutely not! Every child looks up to the mother as a model of how he should behave. Hitting and spanking will only result in negative behaviors which can spill over to the future. Besides, it sends the wrong signals to the child. It creates the notion that punishment and the use of force is alright.

As much as possible you should avoid the tantrums by preventing incidents from blowing into a major scene that will only frustrate the kid.

Here are some ways you can avoid incidents from developing into major tantrums.

Give him a dose of negative attention.

According to some child experts, one of the best ways to deal with temper tantrums is to ignore them - whenever possible. It may come as a shock to you but it really doesn't mean you will totally not respond to the child when he starts acting up.

It is a tactical way of ignoring then attending to the child. It is called negative attention. It involves momentarily ignoring the child (even if he starts screaming) until he calms down. And once he has calmed down you divert his attention by offering him something else other than what he wanted. Toddlers have very short attention span so if you offer a replacement for what he wants he is likely to forget everything else at once. This cushions and lessens the feeling of frustration that comes with not getting what he wants.

Take note though that this approach will only work if you have a strong, positive relationship with your child. To achieve this, make it a habit to praise him or reward him with attention for every positive behavior he shows. This will strengthen the positive relationship between you and your child such that when you ignore him every time he starts acting up, it won't escalate into major scene.

Make him feel he is in control.

If your child feels he has control over things he is not likely to go into tantrums. For example, instead of emphatically telling him to do something give him options. An example of this is instead of saying "take a bath now", you can try asking him "Do you want to take a bath now or would you rather do it after dinner?"

Don't push him if he has reached his limits.

If you know your child is tired, don't push him to do another thing like do an errand for you. You should know your child's limits and must not push him to go beyond that.

Accommodate whenever possible.

You may give in once in a while. You should know better when you will ignore his requests and when not to. If the request is reasonable perhaps you should give in. For consistency, make sure that you don't "give in" by first saying no, and then changing your mind, especially if your child has started whining or screaming. Doing this will encourage the bad behavior! Instead, make up your mind whether you will allow the request or not, and then stick to your response.

Be firm if his safety is at stake.

If your child wants to do something where his safety will be compromised and starts acting up because you forbid him, don't give in. Be firm about it to make him understand that when it come to his safety you are inflexible. What you can do is hold him firmly for a while. It will send him the signal that you are not going to budge.

There are two things you must remember when your kid starts acting up. First, keep your cool. Never lose your temper or feel frustrated. Your kid will sense this and he will only be more frustrated. By staying calm you can assess the situation more clearly and take the most appropriate action for the situation.

Second, you should never reward your toddler's tantrums by giving in to his wishes. It will only make him bolder. Knowing that his tantrums work will encourage him to do it again and again to get what he wants.

Do not reward your child's tantrum by giving in. This will only prove to your little one that the tantrum was effective.

Instead, verbally praise a child for regaining control.

You should not really worry much about your child's tantrums because he will stop on his own when he sees it is not getting him anything. Also, the tantrums will slowly disappear as your child matures.

Chapter 12: Mindset

The research behind mindsets is fairly recent. It has become a key to unlocking why some children love to meet challenges head on, versus kids who quit when something is not super easy. I always hate to hear the statements, "I can't do this", "This is too hard", and "That's not fair". Most of the time these statements come before the student has even attempted the assignment. It is annoying as much as it is sad to hear these comments. This is the moment I realize that I have to work on their mindset before I can ever get to teaching them. Surprisingly, it is not just for students who struggle academically, it is also for students who may be doing extremely well academically. but also for those who excel in academics.

Dr. Carol Dweck has done tons of research in figuring out what separates people and especially kids from pushing through failure and attempting challenging things in life. She has coined the phrases "growth" and "fixed" mindset. These mindsets are categorized by some key actions and responses in kids. The fixed mindset is the thought process that our gifts, intelligence, abilities and traits cannot change. This means that people with this mindset believe that they are good or bad at certain things and that cannot change. An example would be someone who takes an IQ test and believes that their IQ cannot be improved. The growth mindset is opposite and refers to the ability for people to fight adversity, continue to try challenging activities, and believe they can achieve just about anything if they put forth the right effort over the right amount of time. Before you immediately tell yourself that you and your child have a growth mindset, you must remember that this mindset works across different areas in life. This means that you can have the growth mindset about some things but have a very fixed mindset when it comes to other areas in life. A kid may be growth minded in sports but fixed minded in academics. You or your child could have a fixed mindset about the level success you are able to obtain because of where you are currently. Dr. Dweck not only developed this revolutionary idea, she and her team have come up with ways to help kids become more growth minded.

Do Not Affix Labels

You have to work on your child's mindset. This is a daily occurrence. Many times in life we have been known to affix labels to kids. People label them as smart or dumb, bad or good. What we have failed to realize for so long is that these labels deeply effect the actions and thought patterns of children. I have seen kids struggle deeply from labels that were given to them by their parents. This is something that they will probably not tell you because they believe this to be the truth since you said it to them.

I talked to a young boy in the third grade who recently transferred due to fights at his last school, who seemed to continuously find himself in trouble. One day while he was in trouble from something that happened the day before, he was told to move and sit at another table. He did not move at all. Oddly enough he stood up and bent over laying his head on the table out of defiance. As I walked over and talked to him I got to a point where I told him that he is not bad. He shook his head in disagreement and said "my mom says I am bad". I repeated to him, "you are not a bad kid". He shook his head once more in disagreement and told me his mom always says he is bad and that's what people always calls him. I responded, "I know you are not bad, you are a good kid that rough things have happened to in the past". He shook his head this time agreeing with my statement. I continued to speak and reassure him that he is not a bad kid and that he has the power to make the decision of how he will act. He sat down in his seat and looked at me with tears welled up in his eyes. It was as if no one ever believed that he could be better than his past. This is why as parents you cannot affix labels to your child. Do not permanently label them good, bad, smart, or dumb.

Behavioral Communication

You are probably wondering how do you praise or correct your child. Gear your focus towards their behavior when you are praising or correcting. You would naturally think calling your kid smart would be a great thing to do. I would not say it is bad, but it does have a side effect if you are cramming this in your child's head. When kids who excel academically are constantly fed they are smart, they tend to have some real issues with failure or challenges that are not easily overcome. It can result in them saying, "That's stupid" or they will try to belittle something if they cannot understand it easily. These children can exhibit extremely high levels of frustration when they meet failure because they have attached the label of being smart to themselves. This frustration and thought process can lead them to developing behavioral issues such as frequently lashing out or low self-esteem. The failure or challenge has made them identify themselves as dumb or stupid. When kids who do poor academically have been affixed with the label of dumb or stupid, they tend to go one or two ways. They can become very lazy when it comes to doing work or they create behavioral issues such as being overly goofy or finding someone to agitate.

How To Help Your Child With A Fixed Mindset

If you have a child that has a fixed mindset then here are some encouraging ways to help them work pass this mindset. When I work with kids I focus on rewarding them for hard work and strong work ethic. When you encourage your child for their endurance, dedication, and hard work they will learn to adopt that behavior. Let them know that failure is just one more step closer to success. If you study any consistently successful person you will find out that they have failed more than most people could imagine. These successful people do not look at failure as the end but only a step closer to their goal. This idea has to be taught to your child. You can use examples such as Michael Jordan, Oprah Winfrey, and Walt Disney just to name a few who failed many times before they came close to success. When you encourage your child, make sure to be specific on what they have done well.

Grit and Grind

Grit and Grind, the famous terminology used for the Memphis Grizzlies needs to be applied to your child as well. As a parent you are the most important resource that they have growing up and you must help them develop a growth mindset. A mind that allows them to push through difficult circumstances. This goes a long way in the classroom but even further in life.

What You Can Say:

Way to work hard!

Keep up the hard work!

Good job using your brain!

I appreciate your polite good behavior

Stop acting like a fool at school, you know how to follow directions!

Don't yell when we are in public!

What Not To Say:

You are a smart/dumb child

You won't amount to anything

You are such a bad/good kid

Encouraging Words To Say

I know this is challenging but I believe you can do it if you keep trying.

I need you to give me your best effort

Good job showing endurance on that tough homework

The most successful people failed the most times, so keep trying

These can be modified but the gist is to be clear and detailed on the behavior that you are praising or discouraging.

Chapter 13: Confident Child

Considering self-confidence of a child, what is child confidence? This is a question biting out parents mind. Children with high self-esteem will be feeling to be so loved and very competent and develop to a happy and grow to a productive person and also without behavioral issues.

GRABBING CHILDS CONFIDENCE

Building boy's confidence

Experts say that boy's self-confidence may be hindered and be at a high risk because of boys stereotypes, which makes them have feelings when they do not meet their expectations. These feelings make them to have an outlet to express feelings. A developing myth is saying that boys don't have feeling but this is becoming contrary nowadays since boys need much attention today and nursing them to nurture as well.

Boys got impulsive and difficult times in sitting for so long and paying attention in class. Boys always need break for some refreshments before sitting and listening for another session which is ideally different to the girls who can sit for long and pay much attention compared to boys.

Boys also dislike interruptions and criticism repeatedly since this would lower boys esteem so fast and lead to frustrations to the boy child. Not only diminishing boys esteem but also diminishes his class performance and behavior.

Boys when frustrated will cause him to get angry and everybody would be saying that the kid is so angry this will get an impact to the kids mind and could lead him being intuitive and arrogant.

To avoid your young man from throwing insults and getting him frustrated, listen to your boy and in classroom, make schedule for short breaks for refreshment for the young man.

Boys need also to be instilled with survival skills and get out to be exposed to a skillful task which they will come out saying 'we did it' the boy will grow confidence and high self-esteem with also instilling the boy with leadership skills which will come to make them soon to become a leader of his family.

Building girl's confidence

Girls get bored with petty issues and makes them get so frustrated. Girls are tender hearted. Girls like to expose their emotions by crying alone and stay moody.

Different from boys, girl's emotions are easy to note and they often expose their feelings.

Girls like more attention compared to boys. Also girls always want a partner who encourages her and as a mother, you require to be the closest to your girl and promote assertiveness to her so that she can be open and confident to expose her feelings without crying alone but having a seat and talking freely with mother. This will improve your girl's confidence.

Always give praise to the girl. Girls need praises and a partner who can inspire her and tell her she's always doing the right thing. Most girls dislike to be told they are doing the wrong job and this would frustrate them so much making them feel lonely and running thoughts through their mind.

Girls require companions who talk to them their secrets and that is all which will grab her confidence to talk and share ideas and issues she has.

FACING LIFE CHALLENGES

Psychologists and counselors from diverse places can play the major role in this sector. This is by understanding children who are from diverse cultural backgrounds and train them to convert their negativity to a positive mental wellbeing. Parents also require this skill which can be obtained from such articles and magazines. The parent is the person who logistically knows the kid well and has great understanding of a child, but will always need some bit of knowledge from the psychiatrists.

In order for this to happen you need to understand the factors that impact on the mental health and the wellbeing of your toddler. This will help you to support the children's cultural sensitivity and responsively.

Typical issues has been encountered by psychiatrists and they have realized that some of the causes of the community linguistics may be to be caused by the common challenges below;

Migration; resettling to a new place or country will bring you and your children encounter different communities with different perspectives towards some communities and race. Some families might have resettled due to some community problems and in the new place they would be recognized as refugees and be treated in a strange way, whether so friendly or so harsh, it will still impact to your children. Impacts to children might be the interaction of children with other people and the engagement of children with some activities might change.

Trauma; situations that children encounter might as well lead to trauma and may affect the child in getting fear or over anxious for something. Also this would impact a similar behavior to the child which will pass something to the parent whether the child dislikes the place, if it would be migration, or the kid has loved the place. Most often, traumatic experiences are encountered when people are exposed to war or the migration due to some reasons. Different traumatic encounters will definitely affect your kid's classwork performance.

Communication; communication issues can affect greatly a person and especially for kids, they would encounter social isolation since communicating with other people becomes a hard task. The social life of the kid will be altered and the kid would get some behavioral changes like staying silent and at times staying so lonely and for girls you would note them locking themselves in their room and cry.

Discrimination; racism is one of the biggest discriminatory issue experienced with people nowadays. Discrimination lowers self-esteem so much that the kid would even feel left out due to an unavoidable melanin. Mostly you would recognize the kids will keep hiding from places like parties, stay silent in occasions and even never get associated to the other color. The impact would affect studies greatly since the kid would concentrate much on avoiding being discriminated of skin color and also keep recalling incidences which he or she was discriminated and would lose social interaction with people as well as class work.

To value all the cultures and colors will automatically bring respect and bring out great bonds between different races. Ideally, as a parent train your kid to get associated with kids of other races and thus engage them together to bring out close bond to avoid being discriminated because of a race.

Chapter 14: Understanding Your Daughter

As your daughter gets older, it is only normal that you will not always get along very well and you will disagree on a lot of things. You may start to feel that you are fighting far too often with your daughter; you are not imagining things. As mentioned, a lot of adolescents view arguments as a way to express themselves. Your daughter is probably just trying to assert her individuality. Nonetheless, these arguments are not that easy to tolerate.

Experts say that on most occasions, daughters tend to target their mothers with their frustration and anger. Studies have also found that there is a rhythm in the fights and misunderstandings that go on in the mother-daughter relationship. These fights have been observed to occur more in the afternoon or evening when both the mother and daughter come home from a long day.

While the parent tries to reinforce her authority as the parent, the daughter tries to keep her freedom and out-of-sight independence. A parent can ask her daughter too many questions, which her daughter can find annoying. Daughters will react in that very single-minded way that they always do. The daughter may feel like her mother is suspecting her of doing something wrong, not stopping to think that her mother may just be interested in knowing things about her life. On both sides, tensions may arise and this will lead to the inevitable battlefield.

Primary Argument Triggers

Research has shown that arguments between parents and their teen daughters are about the following topics:

**The types of friends their adolescent daughter hangs out with

**Lack of neatness, specifically in her bedroom.

**Her relationship with boys, or certain issues about dating.

**Rules, restrictions and curfews

**Her manner of dressing herself, and particular choices of what she should wear

**Liberties

Causes Of Tension

Aside from these topics, tension may also arise between parents and their daughters from things that have to do with:

**The daughter not taking parental advice

** Daughter's frustration, which may come from her mother's lack of validation for her newfound identity.

** Feelings of disappointment when the daughter fails to get her parents' approval.

** Her identity and the things that she is and isn't not allowed to do.

**Her expression of having her own strong viewpoint.

** The daughter's determination in attempting to change her mother's response to her actions.

** Her attitude of believing that she knows everything and her parents know nothing.

**A mother who simply forgives and forgets tends to be her favorite target.

** She may blame her parents, specifically her mother for her unhappiness.

** The rules and restrictions that her parents impose on her. She tends to view these as a "prison".

** Her attempts to lessen her parents' authority over her.

What You Should Not Do

These can be mediated or can be solved by keeping a cool head. However, there are actions that parents sometimes do that can fire up even more arguments.

These include:

** Thinking that you have to be right all the time.

**Your failure to restrain your emotions and temper within your reason.

** You do not let her express her frustrations when it is necessary.

** You secretly want your daughter to feel guilty for her actions.

**Your choice of battles is unwise.

** Keeping your frustration in check is something you find difficult to do.

** You have no confidence in your daughter's own judgment.

** You fail to recognize the rights of your daughter.

** Connecting with her and her emotions is something that you do not do.

** You fail to see the advantages of having a fair argument.

** You do not listen to her and instead keep on rebutting when it is not needed or unwise to do so.

Why You Should Not Worry Too Much

The things that were listed above may give you and your daughter something to think and talk about. Remember that in dealing with your daughter, you have to be open for conversation.

Although you and your daughter may find it difficult to understand or believe, fighting can be a good thing for your relationship. A fair argument between a parent and a child can:

** Help keep extremely important issues from growing, festering and eventually erupting into a huge fight later on.

** Help you and your daughter release any tension between the two of you and clear the air.

** Assist your daughter in developing her problem-solving skills.

** Serve as a way for you and your daughter to express any concerns, problems or emotions that need attention, and may keep the two of you in a close relationship.

** Help in resolving any issues and in promoting change.

Chapter 15: Your Teen's Right To Make Choices

My granddaughter recently told me she no longer believes in God. She then asked why she has to go to Church since it's all about something she doesn't even believe in.

My sons attended church every Sunday until the day they moved out of my house, and it was completely without an argument.

Thankfully, we live in a small town and their friends attended the same church so it was simply that they got to be with their friends.

I explained to my granddaughter that I can't make her believe in God, but she still has to go to church because it is the right thing to do. I said, "When you asked me to take you to the mall – I did, and when your sister asked for her sports physical I took her because your mom works during business hours, so you must do what I ask you to do because it is the right thing to do". She complied.

If your teen rebels and chooses to not join the family on Sundays – whether it's to go to services or simply a drive to grandma's house you may be forced to take drastic measures.

For example, you may choose to use the same "opting out" technique she used. When she wants you to take her somewhere of great importance to her – you may need to show her how it feels when her driver refuses to transport her to the event of her choice.

If she tries to circumvent your taking her, you are still within your parental rights to refuse permission for her to go. It's certainly will be to your advantage and add pressure if her event of choice is similar to yours in that it's a regularly scheduled occurrence.

If the aforementioned situation is not feasible for you then you may wish to use the exchange program – which is entirely different from the bargaining teens are so used to.

The exchange program is much like getting a drivers license. There are hoops that have to be jumped through prior to being issued a driver permit.

So, when your teen asks you to do something for them, you reply that after _____ has been completed or complied with, then I will be happy to _____ for you.

Having them meet your terms first is key.

That process is a part of being an adult and will go with your child throughout their entire life. For example, once you finish your degree you get a good job; once you have complied with the banks lending terms (a work history and established credit worthiness) you get a loan; once you can prove you have a job then you can rent an apartment.

In the old days we called this, "don't put the cart in front of the horse". There's an order for things to occur, and unfortunately too many parents are doing things for their children before the children have earned the right to have it done.

It is certainly true that you can take the horse to the water, but you can't make the horse drink, so don't force them; however, if the horse gets thirsty enough he will eventually drink!

Chapter 16: We all have bad habits

Constantly improve. I've mentioned this plenty of times before, but no parent is perfect. No parent could ever really hope to be, we don't owe perfection to our children. They learn from our struggle to be better people every day, they learn that the struggle is worth it and they're worth fighting for. That they're worth improving for.

We all have bad habits, things that need work. We can claim to be perfect as much as we want, but it isn't fooling anyone at all. Everyone can improve something. Maybe a bad habit. For me, I'm a fiend for caffeine. Don't talk to me until after my coffee in the morning, especially when I'm sitting down and writing for hours every day. Having a cup of coffee is a nice comforting thing. Something that's come to b

Still. I try to keep it in control. It's to easy to let addictions like that get out of control. Whether its to a substance of your phone. Distractions are easy to get lost in, and cause the loss of attention to your family. It isn't just distractions, though. Most of that is covered in my section of being there. There are tons of ways that everyone can improve and become a better person.

Letting your child see you strive to be a better person, occasionally fail and succeed. It's part of being a person, to struggle and learn to be a better human being. Letting them see how you improve, break bad habits and form healthy ones helps them learn to break the bad habits that they may develop.

Let them see you do the right thing. Let them see you do the wrong thing and then try to make it right. Apologize and help them when they make mistakes. Instill the instinct to constantly improve themselves, that humanity has problems, but we can work on the problems.

Take your children with you to vote. To pay bills. Show them what it's like to live in this world, to exist in this kind of modern world. If they have questions that you can't answer, let them help you research the answer. Kids want to know so much, and even if you don't know, you can teach them how to find the answers that they need.

If you can't help them with a certain bit of homework, let them help you learn what they need to do. Have them teach you. Have them help you research things; the internet is an amazing resource. In fact, you probably used it to pick up this book. I've had to look up countless new methods of doing the same math, because the class was teaching it a different way, watching videos of math teachers speak about it with my child sitting right next to me because the ways I solved these problems aren't the way they're teaching children any more, still, it doesn't matter. Even if I don't know, I know how to find the answer for her.

The point of all of this is letting them see that the world isn't always easy, but they can always work to overcome any obstacle, to fight their way through even the worst of situation. Parents are there to protect children, but honestly, we can't protect them from everything, they need to know that there are some things that they can change and many other things that they can improve and change for themselves.

The only thing any of us has the power to change is ourselves. It's a sad bitter truth, but it is the truth. Changing ourselves, however affects the world around us, and becoming a better person is the best way to help show people how to be a better person.

This doesn't mean becoming a doormat. None of us would be happy if our children just accepted being treated awfully. Part of the improvement is easing out of toxic influences in our lives. Not letting people mistreat us and standing up to not take abuse from others. We wouldn't want our children to learn that it's ok for people to treat them terribly, we should maintain the same kind of attitude in our personal life. Part of becoming a better person is fighting through hard times and protecting oneself from mistreatment.

It's always important to keep in mind the world that we live in when making improvements. This is the world that your children live in too. They have to learn to cope and navigate through it too. Realism must take a part of any positive parenting technique.

Chapter 17: Tips On Best Car Seat Position

Recreational vehicle or RV is designed for adventure and most road safety regulations are not adhered to while designing it. Unlike a school bus or the family car, an RV has only two front seats with the entire back being a dining area, thus as a parent, you are faced with the challenge of choosing the best place to install your child's car seat to ensure comfort and maximum safety. Maximum safety for your child is attained by ensuring the following is done in your RV. First, have the correct seat for your child. Most car manufacture companies have adopted the idea of designing car seats with the appropriate height and weight for children of all ages. Thus as a parent, ensure this seat is installed at your RV at all times. Secondly, make sure the car seat is installed correctly. Lastly, ensure your child is buckled up properly at all times during your trip. Most parents particularly mothers might prefer to hold their children during the journey but the kind of risk you are exposing your child to is enormous. Having your child seated and belted up while traveling gives support to the neck and spine as well as offers cushion during a car crash or collision. Therefore, baby proof your RV by adhering to these three requirements before starting your road trip.

The question of where to safely strap your child is another important concern. The front seat is out of question for all children whether in an RV or any other vehicle. This makes traveling with an RV more complicated since the front seat is the only seat available in an RV. Your child's bones and muscles are neither as strong as yours nor stronger enough to deal with the forces that result from rear end collision which is common with most RVs. Having your child in a front seat increases risk of injury to neck, head and spine which is the leading cause of infant mortality in US today. Further, to ensure your child's safety in a front seat of an RV, it means you must use a lap belt which is built with its on restrain harness. However, this is not possible as most RVs don't have lap belts unless you make a request to have yours be custom made with a lap belt. This will definitely make your RV more expensive than an ordinary rental car which defeats the whole point of using an RV in your road trip. Recently, the Federal Seat Belt Association issued a policy requiring all RVs to have seat belts in the dinette area. Though this has been adhered to, the seat belts do not have occupant crash testing. In other words, they have not been subjected to testing in a real life collision situation thus the risks involved with it are not known. Further, these seats are bolted to wooden frame which can easily break during a collision exposing you and your baby to injuries. Therefore, try installing your baby's seat to the bottom of the cushion in dinette area. First remove the cushion and anchor the seat by using top strap. Then, use the lap belt if available and perch the baby's car seat at the bottom of the cushion. Then remove the bottom cushion and place the car seat on the metal frame below the wooden bench. This might sound complicated but most RVs come with a manual on how to install a car seat. The trick is to ensure that your baby's seat is tied to the strongest element in your RV to ensure maximum stability in case of collision. Always ensure that the baby's or any child related restrain is not installed rear-ward or side-facing in your RV.

As a general guide to baby proofing your RV, ensure latches are installed on all drawers and cabinets in the dinette area to reduce cases of injuries in case of a collision. Make sure all electrical outlets covers are properly installed and keep water temperature below 120 degree at all times. Ensure that you use temporary cabinet locks to reduce unnecessary entry to cabinets without your supervision. Unsupervised entry to cabinets can be dangerous if the child gains access to medicines or chemical substances. In addition, door knob cover should be used to limit entry to bathroom and exit doors. For better night sleep, acquire a lightweight baby travel bed as this will prevent cases of child fall as well as keeping your child in a home environment for more comfort. To recap, an RV can be an adventurous way for a family to take a road trip during the holidays. However, the risks involved in using a RV have long been ignored by major manufacturers. Some families acquire the biggest RVs in the hope of getting more secure but this just gives a false sense of security. Others acquire those with seats installed in the dinette but this as well exposes your family to more risks. The probability of kitchen and wooden cabinets collapsing has not been addressed. However, by following the simple guidelines outlined under Where to safely strap in the car seat and baby proofing your RV, you can build an extra layer of security to your family and more particularly to your children and make your road trip more safe and adventurous.

Chapter 18: How To Develop A Strong-Willed Child

So far you have read about how strong-willed children actually possess natural gifts. But what if your child is not strong-willed? You can encourage him to develop the inquisitive, confident, and dedicated traits necessary for success in life through upbringing, family dynamics, and encouragement.

For one thing, these traits are bred through simple things. Start with a routine where your child has to make a few of his own choices. For example, he needs to decide what to wear to school, what to eat for breakfast, and what to pack for his own lunch.

Also, encourage him to help you with chores. Moms will often say, "If I don't do it myself, it will never get done right." This unfortunate attitude breeds insecurities in your children and fails to teach them how to do things right. Work with him and teach him how you want chores done. He will learn how to keep his own house, yard, and pets when he is older.

If he comes to you for advice, talk him through his problem so that he arrives at a solution himself. Ask him, "How do you think you should best approach this?" When he names a bad solution, ask him, "OK, what could go wrong with that?" Guide him to make his own choices.

Ask him questions and make him perform research. While driving, for instance, you might ask him, "Tell me why the sky is blue." Don't accept an "I don't know" or "Why?" Direct him to find out the answer himself. This teaches him to be inquisitive.

When he claims that something is unfair, ask him why. Allow him to speak out against injustice and have his own opinions. This gives him more of a backbone and strong will as he gets older.

Chapter 19: Setting Boundaries And Responsibility

This particular phrase is more than just about disciplining a child. It sets the stage for the structure of a child's development and mental health. The rod is more than just a tool to administer punishment. The rod in this phrase is also a metaphor for responsibility and consequences. For example, young Jane (sorry Jane) wants a new puppy. She begs her parents for the pet promising to do what needs to be done to care for the pet. Her parents grant her request, and she gets her puppy. For the first several hours, Jane is happy and plays with the puppy but the joy of the new animal soon dies out, and the puppy becomes neglected.

Jane's parents warned Jane that her responsibilities are to feed the puppy and take him for walks every day. Jane begins to understand that caring for the puppy is more than what she had expected. The responsibility of the new dog is overwhelming. Jane starts to complain that the dog is cutting into her play time. The parents remind Jane of how she pleaded for months to get a dog. They remind her that the puppy is now her responsibility, and she needs to take care of the dog.

A chore chart is set up to help Jane remember what she must do to keep the dog. In this situation, Jane learns responsibility, for her new pet. Had the parents given in to Jane's complaints (and we certainly almost did) and returned the dog, Jane would not have learned responsibility. Nor would the parents have had the chance to set boundaries for Jane to teach her about the consequences of her actions.

There are far too many parents who have become enablers.

As parents, we must always do what's right for the child's development regardless of any tantrums or emotional blackmail.

Previous generations knew that boundaries go hand in hand with responsibilities. They learned about the consequences of each and every action. Over the course of time, these lessons seemed to have been misplaced. Children no longer have the boundaries and become unruly because they think that they can complain and not do what they need to do. They become lazy and unproductive then wonder why they are not successful in life.

Some blame must be apportioned to some of us so called experts who in order to sell books or get on Oprah TV come up with all manner of gimmicks that do not work long term and will harm our children's development.

Parenting strong-willed children require a lot of patience and a whole lot of common sense.

So how do you teach an unwilling child responsibility? How can you set boundaries when there are none? These questions are easy to answer if the parent is willing to change how they interact with their child and follow two simple rules.

The first step to applying responsibilities to a child is not to overwhelm them. If you give the child too much, it will set them up for failure. Obviously, the puppy was too much for Jane. The constant care of a dog is sometimes even too much for an adult.

Start the child off with something small that is already a part of their everyday life. A simple chore for them to do would be picking up their toys after they are done playing with them.

Seems simple enough. However, this is by far one of the most challenging chores for a child to grasp but easiest to enforce. The parent sets the responsibility for the child and imposes the burden by administering a consequence should the child neglect to follow the rule. For every chance the parent gives the child to pick up the toys, one toy is taken away. This rule is called "The Rapture Rule." The child will see that the toy is being taken away and will throw a fit. With patience, though, the child will soon be grabbing all the toys so that they are not held captive. Once the child learns about picking up after itself, it becomes easier to administer other responsibilities. And of course over time, the child gains back the toys held hostage during the learning process.

The Rapture Rule will not only help keep the house clean of unwanted clutter; it teaches the child that the parent means business and establishes boundaries for the child/parent relationship. Rules are essential for a child's development. Rules are in place everywhere, and if a child does not see them enforced at home, they will think that rules are not necessary elsewhere.

The second step to incorporating responsibilities and boundaries for an impressionable mind is to up the ante. The phrase "Up the Ante" is popular with the gambling crowd. However, this applies to children as well. If a child is bored, it shows in the child's actions and attitude. They begin to act up and cause chaos at times. Many teachers will state this as well. The child needs to be challenged to grow and learn but not so much that they give up.

So Johnny knows that once he is told to pick up his toys he must listen and obey right away or the toys will be taken away. He complies and puts away his toys. Now he needs something else to do. He needs a routine. Putting away the toys should indicate that playtime is over, and something else is about to start. Johnny's new responsibility after putting away his toys is to help with dinner. Setting the table or help with the cooking.

There are far too many parents that refuse to let the child into the kitchen to help with the preparation of a meal. The parent believes the dangers in the kitchen are too high. However, cooking is one of the few activities that are essential to living. Everyone needs to eat, and there are far too many people these days who don't know how to cook anymore due to the parents not allowing them the time to learn.

Now, of course, everyone knows not to allow a child to play with sharp objects. There are though other things for a child to do in the kitchen. Perhaps stir something or measure something. Both of these responsibilities teach other lessons. Measuring out ingredients builds strong math skills. While stirring introduces the child to chemistry, by flipping pancakes over the child is introduced to physics.

Cooking then becomes a fun responsibility that educates and produces positive as well as delicious outcomes. Helping in the kitchen is the easiest way to establish responsibilities and boundaries in a safe environment and is fun as well as engaging for the child. The boundaries are automatically in place for the child as well and provide direct consequences should the child touch something hot or sharp.

These two rules are universal. No matter how old or young the child is. The enforcement of the Rapture Rule can be for any number of situations. From a teenager's phone being confiscated to using the car. As well as Up the Ante should the child prove him or herself to be responsible. Spider-man comics made the phrase "with great power comes great responsibility" popular and is very true.

There are several tools available to help teach children responsibilities and boundaries. Some parents resort to chore charts and rewards for completing a task or chore. This system is easy to set up and allows for instant gratification since the child can see their progress each day. The chore chart is a very powerful tool for those particular children who are stubborn and hard headed. Seeing the gold star put on the board after they have done the correct actions proves to be a snowball effect. The child wants to continue doing the right thing and get rewarded. There is some speculation about how rewards for doing a good job can hurt a child. This opinion is based on the fact that not everything a child does should be rewarded.

For example, Johnny talks back to his mom. This, of course, is not a good habit to have and many children do go through this stage of rebellion. Apparently, the chore chart isn't made for this kind of behavior or to correct this sort of behavior; this is where boundaries need to be set. Johnny needs structure to know that this type of behavior will get him into trouble. Some parents when dealing with this have a time out chair. Some resort to spanking and others let the child continue without any repercussions for their actions.

When it comes to a disrespectful child the term "spare the rod, spoil the child" comes into play. Only this time, it is the parents' responsibility to correct the child and show the child that they are crossing the boundaries. Whatever way the parent disciplines the child, the child must understand the rules that they are breaking. The parent must explain why they are doing what they are doing. The parent cannot simply say, "because I said so." The child must realize and understand why the spanking is being administered or why the child is sent to time out.

In this day and age, it has become harder to apply and regulate the responsibilities and boundaries for a child. Parents seem to be cornered by outside influences telling them how they should raise their child. Some children are harder to get through to than others. Some children only learn the hard way. Forcing Jane to keep the puppy and take care of it teaches her more than responsibility. It goes beyond setting up boundaries. She learns that hard work has great rewards. That puppy will love her and dub her friend for life. Because Johnny stayed on his sports team, he gained leadership skills and became the hero he saw on television.

No matter the parenting style, each and every child needs love, patience, and understanding. They thrive on discipline. It is no wonder a child will adore the one who punishes them. The lesson may not be clear in the beginning, but down the road it will click, and the child will understand. It is those children who do not have the parent input to set boundaries or give them responsibilities that are led inadvertently down the wrong path.

Granted some children may rebel and out of spite throw out their responsibilities and break down the boundaries set in place for them. The parents' job then is to continue to love them and help guide them. It is not the parents' responsibility to bail them out or make everything right. Although granted, that is the gut instinct of any parent. Tough love is sometimes the only way to get through to the child. That doesn't mean turning a cold shoulder or ignoring them. It just means to stand with them, hold their hand and be there to listen and give advice.

Parents have it hard. Not only do they need to shower their children with love, but they also need to set up rules that are to be written in stone; laws that cannot be broken under any circumstances. The parent must be everything the child needs and doesn't want. The mother, the warden, the police, the bank, the chef, the maid, the teacher and a friend. The movie Nanny McPhee has a great line, which is simple and is true. "If you need me but do not want me I must stay. If you want me but no longer need me, I must go."

Chapter 20: Taking The Assistance Of Therapists Or Specialists

In the most extreme of the conditions, it is possible that the child does not respond to simple treatment methods or strategies. Then, you will need to seek out the right help from the right place. This can be calling for the assistance of therapists and other childcare specialists who are acquainted with this condition. It is always better to go to the ones with ample amount of experience, because then, they will have tested and tried methods of helping most kids. While it might not be the right one for your kid, it can be a start and then you will know what kind of treatments to try with him and what not to.

If your son does not like the commotion in the park and hence does not like an evening walk in the park, then some kids could be slowly brought about to get used to it and then get normalized about it, however, there are also others who will absolutely not respond in the same way and might even throw tantrums in case the condition gets too noisy and unbearable. You will then need to know which exactly suits your kid by the method of experimentation. While having your child go through all that makes you very disappointed at the condition, what you need to focus on is the improvement that will follow in the due course of time. This will usually tend to outweigh any challenges and hurdles that fall on the path of the progress.

Subscribing to the service of a therapist will see great opportunities for your child to improve. The most tested and experimented method in this case is the occupational therapy. You could seek help from such practitioner who will know and understand your kid's condition and suggest the proper therapy accordingly. They will also examine him for the extent and the degree of his condition to determine the rigour of the required therapy. In these cases, you will need to give a detailed description of his behaviour and situation at different places for the therapist to draw a specific schedule and strategy for your child.

These specialists will have had a good number of years of experience in dealing with conditions like these and will have a precise idea of what might work in your child's condition. But, like it was earlier mentioned, do not have false hopes and unrealistic expectations off your child. This will only disappoint you if he does not respond in the expected manner. On the other hand, stay prepared for what is to come and then when he shows any sign of improvement, applaud him for it. This will serve as both, a moral boost for your kid and a sense of accomplishment for you.

There is a great demand for you to be one of those sensory smart parents, who know just about everything about their child's condition. These are parents who have put in a great amount of time and efforts into the research of their child's situation and the appropriate methods to overcome it. If you happen to know one of these parents then you will have all the information you will need to know for getting better results for your kids. Just like them, you will need to be very dedicated to make your child receive the best of the treatments at the hands of the most sincere therapists. Chances are that these sensory smart parents will know and may have been in contact of some of the best therapists and specialists, who are experts in dealing with these situations. Knowing them will bring to your doorstep more than just knowledge about your kid's condition.

There are certain resources that will help your child overcome his sensory issues and step into the more normal zone. Each of the therapists is very well aware of these and will also have access to a lot of these materials. If you have sought out the help of these specialists then you will see them use a number of tactics to secure the attention of your child on different things and games, so that he forgets to spin or stays at one place for longer or will communicate in a better manner. However, it is very important to see that these only push your child to a certain limit that exceeds his comfort level and not anywhere beyond it that might cause him acute discomfort.

Being a smart parent of a kid with sensory disorder, you will have to know the proper nutritional diet, the number of hours of sleep or any other special needs that he might have. If you are not aware of any of these, you could always turn to an expert, an experienced therapist to provide the necessary help that you will need to take care of your child. This will equip you to ensure that your kid is receiving all the benefits that he requires to effectively overcome his condition, with the best resources and people at his disposal.

Chapter 21: How Do I Help My Teenager Navigate Relationships (Friends, Family, Dating, Etc)?

Relationships are the main thing that many teenagers are focused on. Friends, family, and dating are all important parts of a teenager's life. But, due to the changes that everyone goes through, all of these can be difficult to work with. So, knowing how you can help your teenager in the navigation of these topics can be incredibly beneficial.

Friends. Friends are difficult during the teenage years because you aren't exactly sure what everyone is thinking or feeling about the friendships. Your teenager will get really angry at someone one week, and then be best friends with them a couple of weeks later. Of course, your instinct is going to be to protect them from anything negative. But the thing is, you can't be over their shoulder every second of the day.

When dealing with friends, the role that you're going to play is one of support. You need to help your teenager with making the right decisions when it comes to deciding who should be a friend and who should not be. You need to also take care and be supportive of the decisions that they are making. There are times where they may need you to step in (where there is clear manipulation, illegal activity, etc), but most of the time, you may just have to stand back and let them learn how to navigate their friendships. They will get hurt, and you just need to be there so that you can offer your support when those things happen. It will be difficult, but with your help, your teenager can learn which relationships that they should be investing in and which ones that they should not spend their energy on.

In general, it's a lot of talking it out and teaching your teen how they should be treating other people. The saying goes, if you want to have a friend, you need to be a friend. And teaching your teenager how to be a good friend will help them find good friends, as well.

Family. Family is probably the most difficult part of the teenager realm. Why? Because they are still working through what family actually is. Yes, it has always been their parent(s) and any sibling(s) that they may have, but as they grow older, their definition of family may be changing. Some of their friends' families may come into the family definition, or some of their closest friends. One phrase that you need to keep in mind during this time is "friends are the family we get to choose." Just because your child is starting to embrace other people that are not biologically related to you as family, does not mean that they are rejecting their family of birth. Instead, they are expanding their family. Encourage this, but let them know that your family is still important and should be a priority to them.

You also want to make sure that you are giving them a good example of what family should be when they are with your family. Teach them to respect all family members and to love them unconditionally. The more you exemplify this in your home, the better they will be with other members of the family that they create over time. Also teach them to be patient with those that they love; it will go a long way with everyone that becomes part of their extended family.

Dating. This is probably the most interesting type of relationship to try and navigate with your teenager, mainly because different parents will have different views on the whole "dating scene." Some parents will not care if their children date, and even encourage it as a healthy way for them to explore relationships with the opposite gender. Other parents will stop their teenagers from dating until they are 16, or even 18.

No matter what you believe about dating, the important thing about dating is that you ensure that all discussions about it are open and understanding. You cannot belittle them or make them think that they can't come to you about their dating relationships. If you do, your teenager will be more likely to hide their relationships from you, which is an outcome that you don't want. Be willing to listen, and make compromises where they are appropriate.

In order to help your teen understand what dating is about and how it should work, make sure that you get some help from other adults in their life; if you're all giving the same messages, the outcome will be a lot more favorable for everyone involved.

Chapter 22: Your Child's Learning Development

The foundation that shapes children's future starts from the first five years of his life. It is when the child's brain develops. The experiences they go through on those years have direct impact on their learning skills. Talking, reading, writing should be introduced to them this early as they learn more quickly during this time. In addition, love and nurture are needed for them to develop a sense of security and confidence.

Helping Your Toddler Talk

Most children do not need any help with talking. They will start babbling like most toddlers do and eventually, the quantity of words they utter will increase daily. Children's ability to articulate words varies from child to child. Some start talking sooner than other children in their age group. Not to worry though. Just give it time and soon enough, with your help and encouragement, your toddler will soon be saying understandable words and be able to tell you what he wants.

Name Game. When you are with your toddler, you need to use his name as much as you can so he knows that it is his identity. Aside from that, your child should be aware of the names of everything he sees. If you are feeding him, name the spoon, bowl, bib, table, fruit, water, milk and so on. If he's having his playtime, name the blocks, mat, book, house, doll and even the names of the people around you so that your toddler has a name for everything.

Reading Time. If you introduce your child to a lot of words, he gains advantage over his peers and reading is one of the best ways. This will help him have a large vocabulary of words and how to use them, understand that words are made up of smaller sounds and knowing the letters of the alphabet, among others. Reading to your child as often as possible will also set the foundation for when he reads by himself.

Listen to what your baby is saying. Be attentive to what your toddler does when you ask him a question. A smile, a frown or even babble are responses and it is his way to communicate with you. When he babbles, try to talk to him as if you are having a conversation with an adult. Say, 'that is really nice, Robert, I like the color pink too, it's beautiful', to him. If he wants something but you cannot understand what, try pointing to an object you think it might be and see how he responds. Sometimes, it will take time before you can understand him, but do not show body language that implies impatience.

Baby Talk. Your toddler learns to speak clear words faster if you talk to him in a normal way. Although baby talking to your baby may seem more fun, it may just delay his speaking abilities.

Corrections. Avoid correcting your toddler's mispronounced words too often or he may give up trying. Nobody wants to be corrected all the time, even babies. When he uses a wrong word for a particular object, you just need to say the correct name for it. So, if your baby says ball instead of doll, you say 'Oh, you want this ball'? He might not get it the first time or even the second time, but patience is the key.

Learning by Playing: Creative Playtime Activities for Toddlers

Your toddler is still in the stage of learning or understanding how things work. His curiosity motivates him to know about the things new to his knowledge. One way of enhancing your child's imagination is through playing. By listening, touching, looking smelling and tasting, he starts to learn about the world around him. Just let him explore the toys, books or things around him. Avoid saying 'no' every time as this just may make his feel bad.

What's in the bag? With this activity you are teaching your child to recognize objects and its texture just by feeling them. Put various items into a bag and ask your child to put his hand inside it and feel one item. Then you may ask him if it is hard, soft, warm, cold, smooth or rough.

Blocks. There are a number of fun activities with blocks that you can teach your toddler. You can ask him to stack blocks as tall as he can and ask how many blocks did it take. This teaches him simple math. After he had stacked them all up, you can ask him to knock them down and you applaud. This is really fun for toddlers and they usually want to do it again.

Shakers. Let him discover different sounds by shaking various plastic containers filled with rice, pebbles, sand, water or any other items you can think of.

Water fun. In a tub during bath time, toddlers enjoy filling and emptying containers. While he is enjoying the water, teach him the words empty and full while pointing to the containers. Just be sure not to leave your toddler alone in the tub as this is very dangerous.

Play house. Toddlers like to play house or play pretend by the time they are three. You can help them dress up as to what character they want to portray. Your toddler may want to be a farmer in a farmyard. Provide him the feel of the farm. You do not necessarily need to buy farm tools or farm animal toys. You can always improvise. Drawings can really go a long way.

Outdoor play. Playing outdoors with your toddler may mean running, climbing or crawling with him. This is good for toddlers because aside from really enjoying his time, this is also a good form of physical exercise. He can also develop hand and eye coordination. A children's park is a good place to expose your children to an activity like this.

Treasure hunt. Let the toddler search for things that are in pairs inside his play area, for example, a pair of shoes or socks. You can also be more creative by making him search for two or three things having the same color. This will be exciting as well as educating. This teaches the child to categorize, count and to be patient as well.

Play Tag. You chasing each other will make this activity fun for the child and the child at heart. This game will benefit your toddler by building his motor skills as well as social skills.

What's missing? This is done by placing a number of toys in a bag or a hat. Remove one item from the bunch without showing him and ask your toddler which one is missing. This is a good activity as it strengthens his memory skills.

Discovery. Toddlers enjoy opening and closing drawers and pushing buttons on the TV just to see how it works. These are few of the many ways toddlers discover things. Try to avoid saying 'no' to his discovery play. What you can do is, put up a box full of different interesting things, like papers, crayons, sock, cups, books, old playing cards. From time to time, try to place a new thing inside so he gets excited the next time he discovers something he has not seen yet.

Conclusion

The title of step parent does not generally order the appreciation it merits. Actually, step parent have enormous ability to influence positive change in their step kid's life. Try not to be plagued by the generalizations and do not be disheartened by any underlying difficulties. Families, whether blended or biological, are less characterized by bloodlines, rather more they are by affection and appreciation.

Regardless of what the circumstances of your new family, odds are there will be a few blocks along the way. In any case, do not surrender attempting to make things work; regardless of the possibility that things began off somewhat rough, despite everything they can enhance as yourself and your new relatives become more acquainted with each other better.

www.ingramcontent.com/pod-product-compliance
Lightning Source LLC
Chambersburg PA
CBHW072009070526
44583CB00015B/1408